# Mobile Computing

Dr.K. Selvakumar

G. Revathy

**Published by**

**Mobile Computing**

**ISBN 978-93-86176-75-2**

**Authors**

Dr.K. Selvakumar

G. Revathy

**Bonfring**

309, 2nd Floor, 5th Street Extension, Gandhipuram,

Coimbatore-641 012.

Tamilnadu, India.

E-mail: info@bonfring.org

Website: www.bonfring.org

Phone: 0422 4213231

# Preface

Mobile communication plays a pivotal role in global world. A study of mobile communication is, therefore, indispensible for students of engineering in order to excel in networking fields. This book has been written with a view to provide informative information on mobile computing  for the third year BE degree students studying computer science in engineering college affiliated to the anna university steam. This book covers the topic like introduction, mobile transport and protocol layers, mobile telecommunication systems, mobile adhoc networks and mobile applications and platforms. Introduction about mobile computing concepts have been explained in detail in **Chapter 1**. Mobile internet protocol and transport layer along with their applications are covered in **Chapter 2**. **Chapter 3** describes the basics of various types of mobile telecommunication systems and their applications. **Chapter 4** discusses mobile adhoc networks and their applications. **Chapter 5** elucidates mobile platforms along with their applications. The text presents the fundamental principles of mobile computing and their applications in a simple language. A lucid writing style has been followed, which makes easier for students to understand the concepts. Equal attention is devoted to elucidating engineering applications of the various topics in every chapter. To summarize, the salient features of this book are :

- Complete syllabus coverage.
- Simple and lucid writing style.
- Rich pedagogy.

*Dr.K. Selvakumar*
*G. Revathy*

# Acknowledgement

*It is our prime duty to express my gratefulness to the Almighty for the blessings. Without the divine grace and blessings, nothing would have been possible.*

*We feel proud to express my sincere thanks and deep sense of indebtedness to **Vice Chancellor, Registrar and Dean**, Annamalai University, Annamalai nagar, for constructive encouragement in preparation of this book.*

*We humbly place my sincere thanks to **Professor and Head, Department of Information Technology**, for his valuable suggestions to successfully carry out to bring this book.*

*We would like to thank **Controller of Examiner and our department faculty members**, for their extraordinary support in this book process.*

*Last but not least, we would like to express my enormous sense of gratitude and thankfulness to our beloved parents whose blessings have always enabled us to successful in all my endeavors, and also the sterling support of our family in bringing this book.*

# IT6601 MOBILE COMPUTING                                       L T P C 3 0 0 3

## UNIT 1 INTRODUCTION                                                    (9)

Mobile Computing – Mobile Computing Vs wireless Networking – Mobile Computing Applications – Characteristics of Mobile computing – Structure of Mobile Computing Application. MAC Protocols – Wireless MAC Issues – Fixed Assignment Schemes – Random Assignment Schemes – Reservation Based Schemes.

## UNIT 2 MOBILE INTERNET PROTOCOL AND TRANSPORT LAYER          (9)

Overview of Mobile IP – Features of Mobile IP – Key Mechanism in Mobile IP – route Optimization. Overview of TCP/IP – Architecture of TCP/IP- Adaptation of TCP Window – Improvement in TCP Performance

## UNIT 3 MOBILE TELECOMMUNICATION SYSTEM                                 (9)

Global System for Mobile Communication (GSM) – General Packet Radio Service (GPRS) – Universal Mobile Telecommunication System (UMTS).

## UNIT 4 MOBILE AD-HOC NETWORKS                                          (9)

Ad-Hoc Basic Concepts – Characteristics – Applications – Design Issues – Routing – Essential of Traditional Routing Protocols –Popular Routing Protocols – Vehicular Ad Hoc networks ( VANET) – MANET Vs VANET – Security.

## UNIT 5 MOBILE PLATFORMS AND APPLICATIONS                               (9)

Mobile Device Operating Systems – Special Constrains & Requirements – Commercial Mobile Operating Systems – Software Development Kit: iOS, Android, BlackBerry, Windows Phone – M-Commerce – Structure – Pros & Cons – Mobile Payment System – Security Issues.

## Text Book

1. Prasant Kumar Pattnaik and Rajib Mall, "Fundamentals of Mobile Computing", PHI Learning Pvt. Ltd, New Delhi, 2012.

## References

1. Jochen H. Schller, "Mobile Communications", Second Edition, Pearson Education, New Delhi, 2007.
2. Dharma Prakash Agarval, Qing and An Zeng, "Introduction to Wireless and Mobile systems", Thomson Asia Pvt Ltd, 2005.

3. Uwe Hansmann, Lothar Merk, Martin S. Nicklons and Thomas Stober, "Principles of Mobile Computing", Springer, 2003.
4. William C.Y. Lee, "Mobile Cellular Telecommunications-Analog and Digital Systems", Second Edition, Tata Mc Graw Hill Edition, 2006.
5. C.K. Toh, "AdHoc Mobile Wireless Networks", First Edition, Pearson Education, 2002.
6. Android Developers : http://developer.android.com/index.html
7. Apple Developer : https://developer.apple.com/
8. Windows Phone Dev Center : http://developer.windowsphone.com
9. BlackBerry Developer : http://developer.blackberry.com/

# UNIT -1

## INTRODUCTION

## 1.1    Mobile Computing

It is a technology that allows transmission of data, voice and video via a computer or any other wireless enabled device without having to be connected to a fixed physical link.

## 1.2    Mobile Computing vs Wireless Networking

The terms "mobile" and "wireless" are often used interchangeably but in reality, they are two very different concepts applied to modern computing and technology.

Mobile is a word that is commonly used to describe portable devices. A mobile device is one that is made to be taken anywhere.

Therefore, it needs an internal battery for power, and must be connected to a modern mobile network that can help it to send and receive data without attaching to a hardware infrastructure.

Wireless, on the other hand, does not mean mobile. Traditional computers or other non-mobile devices can access wireless networks. One very common example is the use of a localized browser product in a local area network (LAN), where the router takes what used to be a cabled interaction and makes it wireless.

Other kinds of wireless networks called wide area networks (WAN) can even use components of 3G or 4G wireless systems made specifically for mobile devices, but that doesn't mean that the devices on these networks are mobile. They may still be plugged in or require proximity to a router or network node.

Mobile and wireless systems really accomplish two very different things. While a wireless system provides a fixed or portable endpoint with access to a distributed network, a mobile system offers all of the resources of that distributed network to something that can go anywhere, barring any issues with local reception or technical area coverage.

For another example of the difference between mobile and wireless, think of businesses that offer Wi-Fi hotspots. A Wi-Fi hotspot is typically a resource for someone who has a relatively fixed device, such as a laptop computer that doesn't have its own internal Internet access built in.

By contrast, mobile devices already have inherent access to the Internet or other wireless systems through those cell tower networks that ISPs and telecom companies built specifically for them. So mobile devices don't need Wi-Fi-they already have their connections.

## 1.3    Mobile Computing Application

These are the following application

a) Vehicles

b) Business

c) Emergencies

1.  Vehicles

   - transmission of news, road condition, weather, music via DAB

   - personal communication using GSM

   - position via GPS

   - local ad-hoc network with vehicles close-by to prevent accidents, guidance system, redundancy

   - vehicle data (e.g., from busses, high-speed trains) can be transmitted in advance for maintenance

2.  Medical

   - Nurses/Doctors in Medical offices are now using Wireless Tablet PCs/WLAN to collect and share patient information.

3.  Sales/ Business

   - Sales representatives are using Tablet PCs with Smart phones for presentation, transmitting/access information among office, hotel, and customer location.

4.  Emergencies

   - Early transmission of patient data to the hospital, current status, first diagnosis

   - Provide mobile infrastructure in dealing with Natural Disaster (earthquake, hurricane, fire), terrorist attacks, war...

## 1.4    Characteristic of Mobile Computing

A computing environment is said to be mobile when either the sender or the receiver of the information is moving while transmitting.

Given below is the list of application.

a) Ubiquity

b) Location awareness

c) Adaption

d) Broadcast

e) Personalization

Lets see the explanation for each

## a) Ubiquity

It means "present everywhere". In mobile computing the ability of a user to perform computation from anywhere and at anytime. Eg: a business executive can receive business notification and issue business transaction as long he is in the wireless coverage area.

## b) Location Awareness

A handeld device equipped with global positioning system (GPS) can transparently provide information about the current location of a user to a tracking station. For example,

- A person travelling by car may easily find out the car maintenance by using the application.
- Other application like traffic control, fleet management and emergency service.
  1. Traffic control–The density of the traffic along the roads can be monitored.
  2. Fleet management-The manager of the transport company can have up-to-date information regarding the position of its fleet vehicles.
  3. Emergency service–Directing the emergency vehicle to the place of call.

## c) Adaption

The ability of the system to adjust to bandwidth fluctuation without the knowledge of the user.

## d) Broadcast

Due to the broadcast nature there is a efficient delivery of data can be made simultaneously to thousands of mobile users.

## e) Personalization

Services in a mobile environment can be easily personalized according to a user's profile. This is required to let the user get the information easily in their hand held device.

## 1.5    Structure of Mobile Computing Application

The structure is usually in terms of functionalities implementation. It is three-tie structure of a mobile computing application shown n fig 1.1.

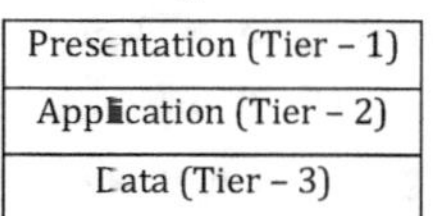


Fig.1.1: Three-tie Mobile Computing Application

Now consider an sales example and we will apply in this three tier application. Below is the fig 1.2 which shows how the sales example is implemented in it.

### *Presentation Tier*

The topmost level of a mobile computing application concern the user interface. A good user interface facilities the users to issue request and to present the result to them meaningfully. The programs at this layer run on the client's computer. This layer usually includes web browsers and customized client programs for dissemination of information and for collection of data from the user.

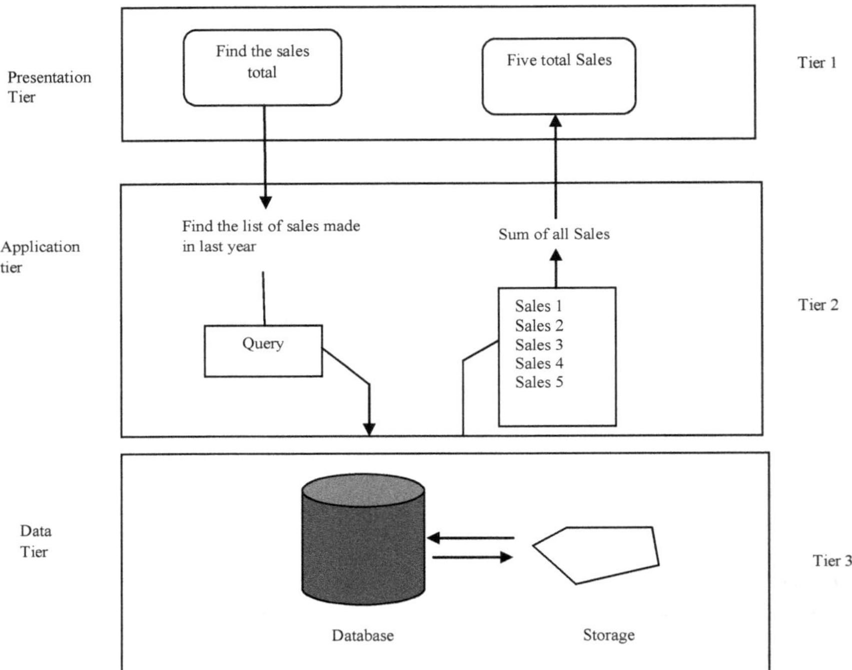


Fig. 1.2: Structure of Mobile Computing Application

### *Application Tier*

This layer has the vital responsibility of making logical decision and performing calculation. It also moves and processes data between the presentation and data layers. It performs the processing of user input, obtaining information and then making decision. This layer is implementation using technology like Java, .NET services, cold fusion, etc. The implementation of this layer and the functionality provided by this layer should be database independent. This layer of functionalities is usually implemented on a fixed server.

***Data Tier***

The data tier is responsible for providing the basic facilities of data storage, access and manipulation. Often this layer contains a database. The information is stored and retrieved from this database. But, when only small amount of data need to be stored , a file system can be used. This layer is also implemented on a fixed server.

## 1.6    MAC Protocols

***What is MAC?***

The *medium access control or media access control(MAC)* layer is the lower sublayer of the data link layer (layer 2) of the seven-layer OSI model. The MAC sublayer provides addressing and channel access control mechanisms that make it possible for several terminals or network nodes to communicate within a multiple access network that incorporates a shared medium, e.g. an Ethernet network. The hardware that implements the MAC is referred to as a media access controller. Figure 1.3 shows the MAC layer.

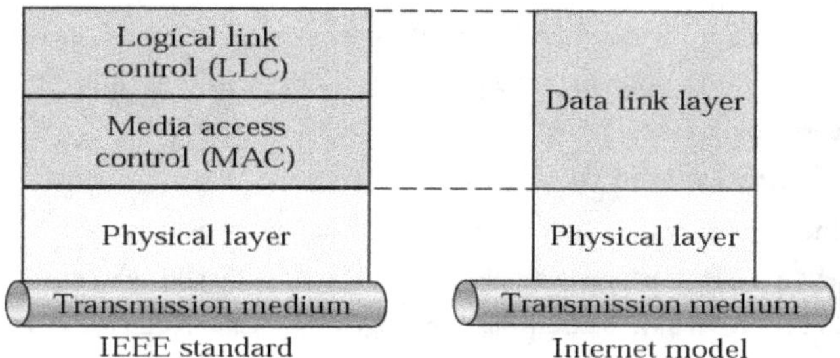


Fig. 1.3: MAC

***Function Performed BT MAC Sublayer***

- Frame delimiting and recognition
- Addressing of destination stations (both as individual stations and as groups of stations)
- Conveyance of source-station addressing information
- Transparent data transfer of LLC PDUs, or of equivalent information in the Ethernet sublayer
- Protection against errors, generally by means of generating and checking frame check sequences
- Control of access to the physical transmission medium

### *Motivation for a Specialized MAC*

One of the most commonly used MAC schemes for wired networks is carrier sense multiple access with collision detection (CSMA/CD). In this scheme, a sender senses the medium (a wire or coaxial cable) to see if it is free. If the medium is busy, the sender waits until it is free. If the medium is free, the sender starts transmitting data and continues to listen into the medium. If the sender detects a collision while sending, it stops at once and sends a jamming signal. But this scheme doest work well with wireless networks. The problems are:

- Signal strength decreases proportional to the square of the distance
- The sender would apply CS and CD, but the collisions happen at the receiver
- It might be a case that a sender cannot "hear" the collision, i.e., CD does not work
- Furthermore, CS might not work, if for e.g., a terminal is "hidden"

## 1.7    Wireless MAC Protocols : Some Issues

This Mac protocols is complex to implement than wired one. A collision detection scheme is difficult to implement in a wireless environment since collision are hard to be detected by the transmission node. The issues of hidden and exposed terminal make a MAC protocol extremely inefficient unless special care is taken to overcome these problems.

### *1.7.1    Hidden and Exposed Terminals*

Consider the scenario with three mobile phones as shown below. The transmission range of A reaches B, but not C (the detection range does not reach C either). The transmission range of C reaches B, but not A. Finally, the transmission range of B reaches A and C, i.e., A cannot detect C and vice versa. Fig 1.4 illustrates this.

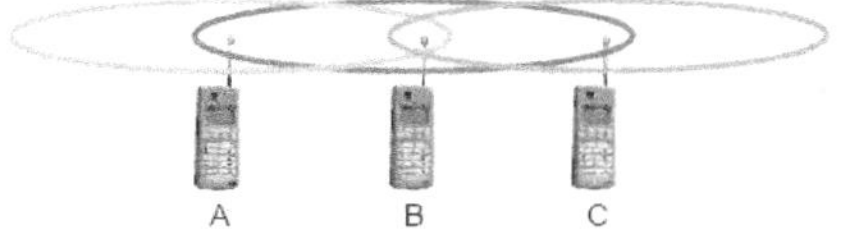


Fig. 1.4: Hidden and Exposed Terminal

### *Hidden Terminals*

- A sends to B, C cannot hear A.
- C wants to send to B, C senses a "free" medium (CS fails) and starts transmitting.
- Collision at B occurs, A cannot detect this collision (CD fails) and continues with its transmission to B.
- A is "hidden" from C and vice versa.

### *Exposed Terminals*

- B sends to A, C wants to send to another terminal (not A or B) outside the range
- C senses the carrier and detects that the carrier is busy.
- C postpones its transmission until it detects the medium as being idle again
- but A is outside radio range of C, waiting is not necessary
- C is "exposed" to B

Hidden terminals cause collisions, where as Exposed terminals causes unnecessary delay.

### *1.7.2 Near and Far Terminals*

Consider the situation shown below. A and B are both sending with the same transmission power. Fig 1.5 illustrates this

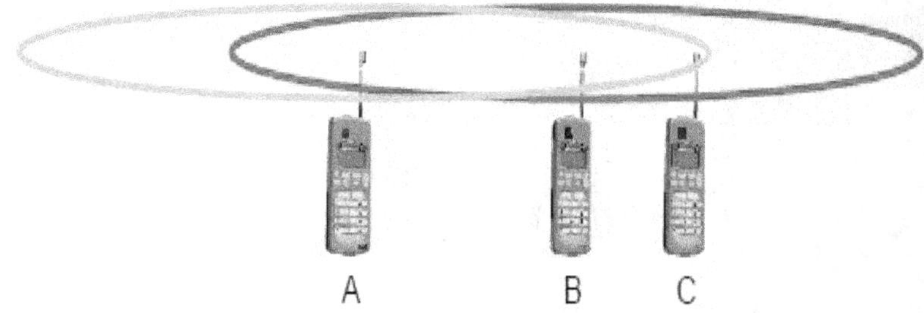

Fig. 1.5: Near and Far Terminals

- Signal strength decreases proportional to the square of the distance
- So, B's signal drowns out A's signal making C unable to receive A's transmission
- If C is an arbiter for sending rights, B drown out A's signal on the physical layer making C unable to hear out A.

The **near/far effect** is a severe problem of wireless networks using CDM. All signals should arrive at the receiver with more or less the same strength for which Precise power control is to be implemented.

## 1.8 Taxonomy of MAC Protocols

A large number of protocols have been proposed. These MAC protocols can be broadly divided into the following three categories.

- Fixed Assignment Scheme
- Random Assignment Scheme
- Reservation Based Scheme

# 1.9    Fixed Assignment Scheme

This scheme is also called **circuit–switched scheme**. Here the resources required for a call are assigned for the entire duration of the call. A few important categories of fixed assignment MAC protocols are the following:

- Frequency Division Multiple Access (FDMA)
- Time Division Multiple Access (TDMA)
- Code Division Multiple Access (CDMA)

### *1.9.1   FDMA*

FDMA is the process of dividing one channel or bandwidth into multiple individual bands, each for use by a single user (Fig. 1.6). Each individual band or channel is wide enough to accommodate the signal spectra of the transmissions to be propagated. The data to be transmitted is modulated on to each subcarrier, and all of them are linearly mixed together.

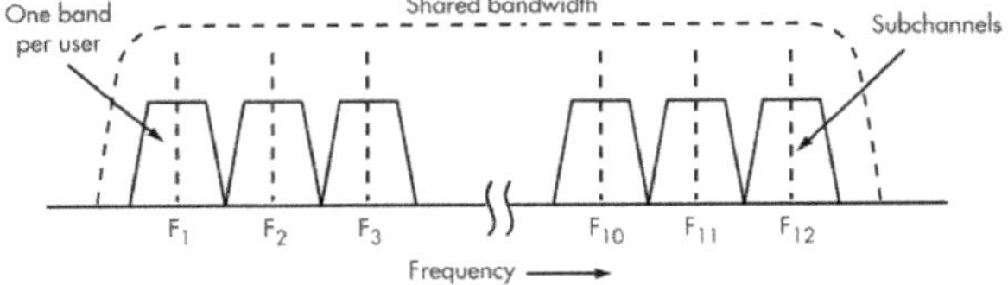


Fig. 1.6: FDMA

*FDMA divides the shared medium bandwidth into individual channels. Subcarriers modulated by the information to be transmitted occupy each subchannel.*

The best example of this is the cable television system. The medium is a single coax cable that is used to broadcast hundreds of channels of video/audio programming to homes. The coax cable has a useful bandwidth from about 4 MHz to 1 GHz. This bandwidth is divided up into 6-MHz wide channels. Initially, one TV station or channel used a single 6-MHz band. But with digital techniques, multiple TV channels may share a single band today thanks to compression and multiplexing techniques used in each channel.

This technique is also used in fiber optic communications systems. A single fiber optic cable has enormous bandwidth that can be subdivided to provide FDMA. Different data or information sources are each assigned a different light frequency for transmission. Light generally isn't referred to by frequency but by its wavelength ($\lambda$). As a result, fiber optic FDMA is called wavelength division multiple access (WDMA) or just wavelength division multiplexing (WDM).

One of the older FDMA systems is the original analog telephone system, which used a hierarchy of frequency multiplex techniques to put multiple telephone calls on single line. The analog 300-Hz to 3400-Hz voice signals were used to modulate subcarriers in 12 channels from 60 kHz to 108 kHz. Modulator/mixers created single sideband (SSB) signals, both upper and lower sidebands. These subcarriers were then further frequency multiplexed on subcarriers in the 312-kHz to 552-kHz range using the same modulation methods. At the receiving end of the system, the signals were sorted out and recovered with filters and demodulators.

Original aerospace telemetry systems used an FDMA system to accommodate multiple sensor data on a single radio channel. Early satellite systems shared individual 36-MHz bandwidth transponders in the 4-GHz to 6-GHz range with multiple voice, video, or data signals via FDMA. Today, all of these applications use TDMA digital techniques.

### *1.9.2   TDMA*

TDMA is a digital technique that divides a single channel or band into time slots. Each time slot is used to transmit one byte or another digital segment of each signal in sequential serial data format. This technique works well with slow voice data signals, but it's also useful for compressed video and other high-speed data.

A good example is the widely used T1 transmission system, which has been used for years in the telecom industry. T1 lines carry up to 24 individual voice telephone calls on a single line (Fig.1.7 ). Each voice signal usually covers 300 Hz to 3000 Hz and is digitized at an 8-kHz rate, which is just a bit more than the minimal Nyquist rate of two times the highest-frequency component needed to retain all the analog content.

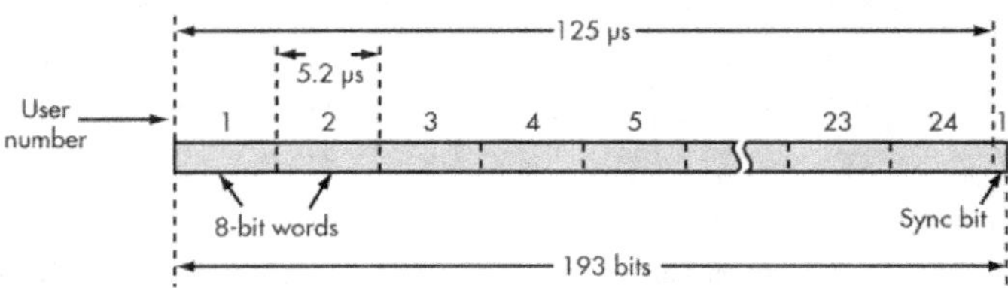


Fig. 1.7: TDMA

*This T1 digital* telephony *frame illustrates TDM and TDMA. Each time slot is allocated to one user. The high data rate makes the user unaware of the lack of simultaneity.*

The digitized voice appears as individual serial bytes that occur at a 64-kHz rate, and 24 of these bytes are interleaved, producing one T1 frame of data. The frame occurs at a 1.536-MHz rate (24 by 64 kHz) for a total of 192 bits. A single synchronizing bit is added for timing purposes for an overall data rate of 1.544 Mbits/s. At the receiving end, the individual voice bytes are recovered at the 64-kHz rate and passed through a digital-to-analog converter (DAC) that reproduces the analog voice.

The basic GSM (Global System of Mobile Communications) cellular phone system is TDMA-based. It divides up the radio spectrum into 200-kHz bands and then uses time division techniques to put eight voice calls into one channel. Figure 1.8  shows one frame of a GSM TDMA signal. The eight time slots can be voice signals or data such as texts or e-mails. The frame is transmitted at a 270-kbit/s rate using Gaussian minimum shift keying (GMSK), which is a form of frequency shift keying (FSK) modulation.

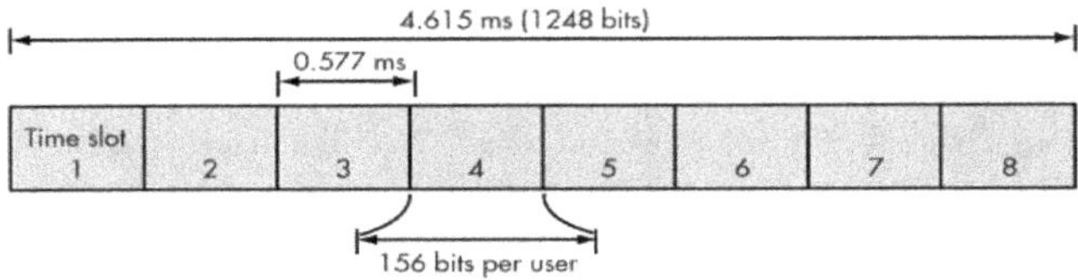

Fig. 1.8: Frame of a GSM TDMA Signal

*This GSM digital cellular method shows how up to eight users can share a 200-kHz channel in different time slots within a frame of 1248 bits.*

### 1.9.3   CDMA

CDMA is another pure digital technique. It is also known as spread spectrum because it takes the digitized version of an analog signal and spreads it out over a wider bandwidth at a lower power level. This method is called direct sequence spread spectrum (DSSS) as well (Fig. 1.9). The digitized and compressed voice signal in serial data form is spread by processing it in an XOR circuit along with a chipping signal at a much higher frequency. In the cdma IS-95 standard, a 1.2288-Mbit/s chipping signal spreads the digitized compressed voice at 13 kbits/s.

The chipping signal is derived from a pseudorandom code generator that assigns a unique code to each user of the channel. This code spreads the voice signal over a bandwidth of 1.25 MHz. The resulting signal is at a low power level and appears more like noise. Many such signals can occupy the same channel simultaneously. For example, using 64 unique chipping codes allows up to 64 users to occupy the same 1.25-MHz channel at the same time. At the receiver, a correlating circuit finds and identifies a specific caller's code and recovers it.

The third generation (3G) cell-phone technology called wideband CDMA (WCDMA) uses a similar method with compressed voice and 3.84-Mbit/s chipping codes in a 5-MHz channel to allow multiple users to share the same band.

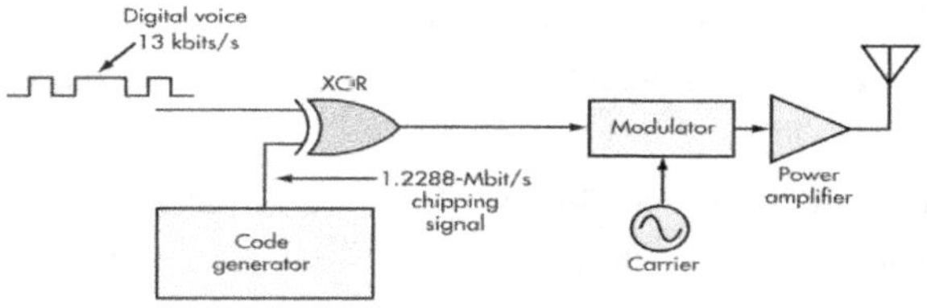


Fig. 1.9: CDMA

*Spread spectrum is the technique of CDMA. The compressed and digitized voice signal is processed in an XOR logic circuit along with a higher-frequency coded chipping signal. The result is that the digital voice is spread over a much wider bandwidth that can be shared with other users using different codes.*

## 1.10  Random Assignment Scheme

This is also called packet–switched scheme. It is compared to the connectionless packet switching scheme. Here no resource reservations are made; the nodes start to transmit as soon as the packet are available. Many scheme are available , few are listed here

- ALOHA
- Slotted ALOHA
- CSMA
- CSMA/CD
- CSMA/CA

### *1.10.1  Aloha*

In this scheme, TDM is applied without controlling medium access. Here each station can access the medium at any time as shown n fig 1.10:

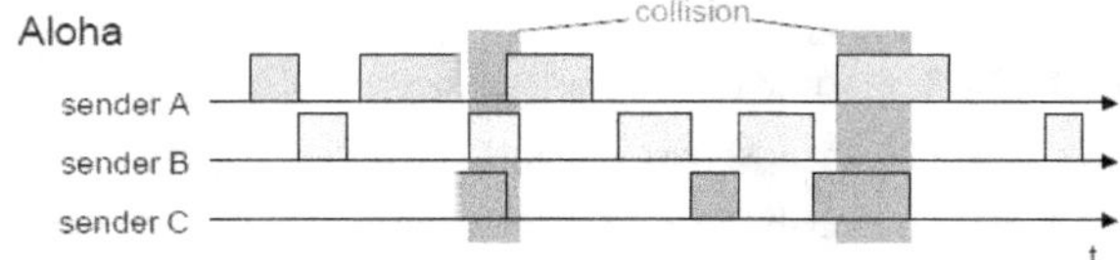


Fig. 1.10: Aloha

This is a random access scheme, without a central arbiter controlling access and without coordination among the stations. If two or more stations access the medium at the same time, a **collision** occurs and the transmitted data is destroyed. Resolving this problem is left to higher layers (e.g., retransmission of data). The simple Aloha works fine for a light load and does not require any complicated access mechanisms.

### *1.10.2 Slotted Aloha*

The first refinement of the classical Aloha scheme is provided by the introduction of time slots (**slotted Aloha**). In this case, all senders have to be **synchronized**, transmission can only start at the beginning of a **time slot** as shown in fig 1.11.

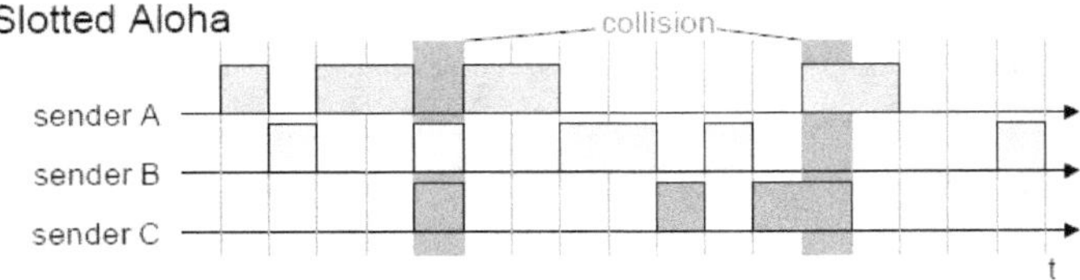


Fig. 1.11: Slotted Aloha

The introduction of slots raises the throughput from 18 per cent to 36 per cent, i.e., slotting doubles the throughput. Both basic Aloha principles occur in many systems that implement distributed access to a medium. Aloha systems work perfectly well under a light load, but they cannot give any hard transmission guarantees, such as maximum delay before accessing the medium or minimum throughput.

### *1.10.3 Carrier Sense Multiple Access*

One improvement to the basic Aloha is sensing the carrier before accessing the medium. Sensing the carrier and accessing the medium only if the carrier is idle decreases the probability of a collision. But, as already mentioned in the introduction, hidden terminals cannot be detected, so, if a hidden terminal transmits at the same time as another sender, a collision might occur at the receiver. This basic scheme is still used in most wireless LANs. The different versions of CSMA are:

- **1-persistent CSMA**: Stations sense the channel and listens if its busy and transmit immediately, when the channel becomes idle. It's called 1-persistent CSMA because the host transmits with a probability of 1 whenever it finds the channel idle.

- **Non-persistent CSMA**: stations sense the carrier and start sending immediately if the medium is idle. If the medium is busy, the station pauses a random amount of time before sensing the medium again and repeating this pattern.

- **p-persistent CSMA**: systems nodes also sense the medium, but only transmit with a probability of p, with the station deferring to the next slot with the probability 1-p, i.e., access is slotted in addition

CSMA with collision avoidance (**CSMA/CA**) is one of the access schemes used in wireless LANs following the standard IEEE 802.11. Here sensing the carrier is combined with a back-off scheme in case of a busy medium to achieve some fairness among competing stations. Fig 1.12 explain it .

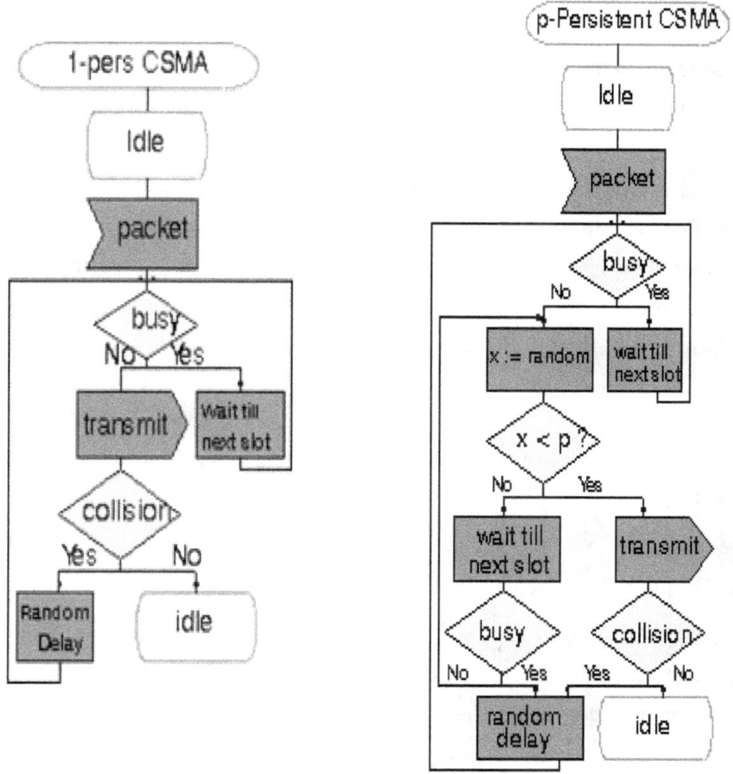


Fig. 1.12: CSMA

## 1.11  Reservation Based Scheme

A basic form of the reservation scheme is the RTS/CRS scheme. Here the sender transmits an RTS(Ready to Send) packets to the receiver before the actual data transmission. On receiving, the receiver sends a CTS (Clear to send) packet , and the actual data transfer commences only after that. When the other nodes sharing the medium sense the CTS packets, theu refrain from transmitting unitl the transimission from the sender node is complete.

A few examples of RTC – CTS based on MAC protocols are

- MACA
- MACAW
- MACA-BI
- PAMAS

### 1.11.1  MACA-Collision Avoidance

MACA (Multiple Access with Collision Avoidance) uses short signaling packets for collision avoidance

- RTS (request to send): a sender request the right to send from a receiver with a short RTS packet before it sends a data packet
- CTS (clear to send): the receiver grants the right to send as soon as it is ready to receive

Signaling packets contain

- sender address
- receiver address
- packet size

Variants of this method can be found in IEEE802.11 as DFWMAC (Distributed Foundation Wireless MAC)

### MACA Examples

MACA avoids the problem of hidden terminals

- A and C want to send to B
- A sends RTS first
- C waits after receiving CTS from B

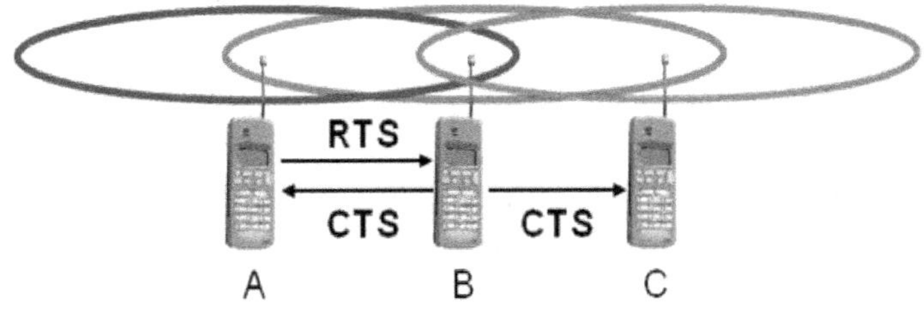


Fig. 1.13: MAC Example

MACA avoids the problem of exposed terminals

- B wants to send to A, C to another terminal
- now C does not have to wait for it cannot receive CTS from A

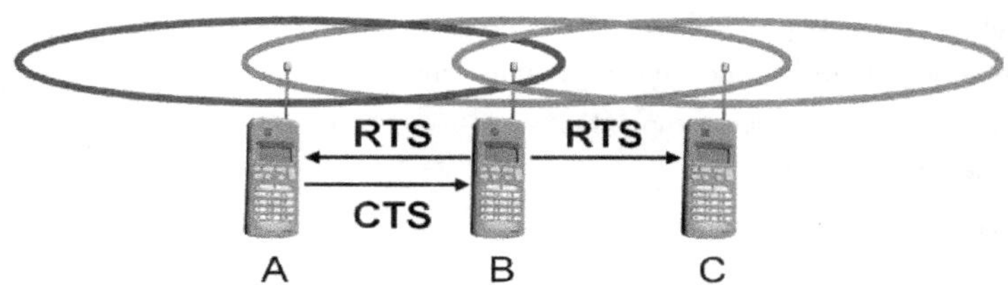


## 1.12   Comparison between SDMA, TDMA, FDMA and CDMA

| Approach | SDMA | TDMA | FDMA | CDMA |
|---|---|---|---|---|
| Idea | segment space into cells/sectors | segment sending time into disjoint time-slots, demand driven or fixed patterns | segment the frequency band into disjoint sub-bands | spread the spectrum using orthogonal codes |
| Terminals | only one terminal can be active in one cell/one sector | all terminals are active for short periods of time on the same frequency | every terminal has its own frequency, uninterrupted | all terminals can be active at the same place at the same moment, uninterrupted |
| Signal separation | cell structure, directed antennas | synchronization in the time domain | filtering in the frequency domain | code plus special receivers |
| Advantages | very simple, increases capacity per km² | established, fully digital, flexible | simple, established, robust | flexible, less frequency planning needed, soft handover |
| Dis-advantages | inflexible, antennas typically fixed | guard space needed (multipath propagation), synchronization difficult | inflexible, frequencies are a scarce resource | complex receivers, needs more complicated power control for senders |
| Comment | only in combination with TDMA, FDMA or CDMA useful | standard in fixed networks, together with FDMA/SDMA used in many mobile networks | typically combined with TDMA (frequency hopping patterns) and SDMA (frequency reuse) | still faces some problems, higher complexity, lowered expectations; will be integrated with TDMA/FDMA |

## Review Questions

### *Part A*

1.   What is mobile computing?
2.   List any 2 difference between mobile computing and wireless network.
3.   Given some of the application of mobile computing.
4.   Draw the structure of mobile computing.
5.   What is MAC?
6.   Define FDMA.
7.   Define TDMA
8.   Define CDMA
9.   What is fixed assignment scheme?
10.  What is random assignment scheme?
11.  What is reservation based assignment scheme?

### *Part B*

1.   List and explain various MAC protocols.
2.   What is mobile computing, give it application and characteristics.

# Unit-2

# Mobile Internet Protocol and Transport Layer

## 2.1.  Overview of Mobile IP

*Mobile IP (or MIP)* is an Internet Engineering Task Force (IETF) standard communications protocol that is designed to allow mobile device users to move from one network to another while maintaining a permanent IP address. Mobile IP for IPv4 is described in IETF RFC 5944, and extensions are defined in IETF RFC 4721. **Mobile IPv6**, the IP mobility implementation for the next generation of the Internet Protocol, IPv6, is described in RFC 6275.

Mobile IP is a modification to IP that allows nodes to receive datagrams no matter where the node is connected to the Internet. This is not possible using normal IP routing because datagrams will always be delivered to the network where IP routing functions would expect to find the node. The solution is an agent at the home network that intercepts datagrams for the Mobile Node (MN) and forwards these to the Mobile Node's current point of attachment.

The Mobile IP protocol was designed with the following goals in mind:

- A Mobile Node must be able to communicate with other nodes after changing its link-layer point of attachment to the Internet without changing its IP address.

- A Mobile Node must be able to communicate with nodes that do not support the Mobile IP protocol. Thus no changes are necessary in the "normal" nodes and routers of the Internet.

- All messages sent to inform about the location of a Mobile Node must be authenticated to prevent redirection attacks.

- The administrative messages sent by a Mobile Node to the other entities should be minimized to save bandwidth.

- No additional constraints must be placed on the assignment of IP addresses. Mobile IP must function using normal IP addresses.

Mobile IP is designed to allow a Mobile Node (MN) to change its location from one IP net to another. There is no constraint on the underlying media, it is thus entirely possible for a MN to move from an IEEE 802.3 LAN to an IEEE 802.11 LAN. Mobile IP is designed to allow the MN to change its point of attachment once a second, the protocol should work for even more frequent moves provided that the MN does not move faster than the roundtrip times for the necessary registrations. Mobile IP thus solves the macro mobility management problem, allowing MN to move between different IP nets and across different link-layers. Still there can be some mobility support in the link layer, for example, does the IEEE 802.11 standard allow a mobile station to roam between access points. Mobile IP works fine with the IEEE 802.11 standard. For example, in a setting where the IEEE 802.11 standard provides mobility between different access points in the same IP subnet and Mobile IP provides mobility when the MN moves between IP nets.

The Mobile IP protocol has the following three functional entities:

- A **Mobile Node (MN)** is a host or router that changes its point of attachment to the Internet.
- A **Home Agent (HA)** is a router on the Mobile Node's home network that maintain information about the Mobile Node's current point of attachment and forwards datagram to the Mobile Node when it is away from the home network.
- A **Foreign Agent (FA)** is a router on a Mobile Node's visited network that provides routing services to the Mobile Node while registered.

The functions needed in the base Mobile IP protocol can be summarized as follows:

- Agent Discovery is the process of the MN discovering whether or not a FA or HA is present. If the HA is present, the MN knows that it is connected to its home network. The MN is able to find the FA or HA through agent advertisements which are an extension to the Router Advertisements of the ICMP protocol.
- Registration is used when a MN that is away from home registers with its HA to let the HA keep track of the current point of attachment of the MN. This registration may be performed by the MN itself or a FA depending on how the MN is connected to the foreign network.
- Tunnelling allows datagram to be sent from the HA to the MN without changing the endpoint addresses of the MN's connections. Datagram may be tunnelled directly to the MN or to the FA that it is currently registered with.
- The typical scenario of the protocol is as follows. The MN arrives at a foreign network and obtains a care-of address, which is the address that is used as the endpoint of the tunnel between the HA and the MN. The care-of address must be an IP address reachable from the HA. A care-of address can either be collocated or the address of a FA.
- A foreign agent care-of address is the address of a FA provided by the FA to the MN through the use of agent advertisement messages. The FA acts as the endpoint of the tunnel with the HA in the other end. The FA de capsulate all arriving datagram from the tunnel and delivers them to the MN.

- A collocated care-of address is an IP address, obtained either statically or through the use of DHCP that the MN uses as the endpoint of the tunnel with the HA in the other end. In this case the MN de capsulates the tunnelled datagram itself.

After the MN has obtained a care-of address, it registers this with its HA. This lets the HA keep track of where to tunnel datagrams destined for the MN. When the MN register with the HA, the HA uses proxy ARP or gratuitous ARP to associate the MN's IP address with the HA's link-layer address. This means that all datagrams destined for the MN will be delivered to the HA, the HA then tunnels incoming datagrams to the MN's care-of address.

When the MN sends datagrams it just does so using normal IP routing. This pattern is called triangular routing, because the traffic flows in a triangle see figure2.1 that depicts the traffic flow without a foreign agent.

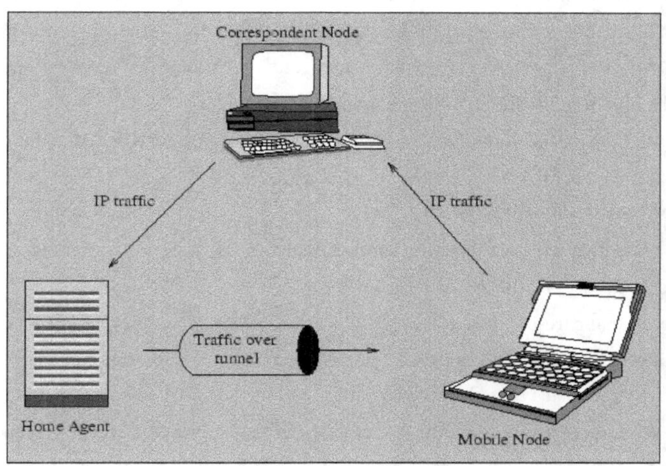


Fig. 2.1: Triangular Routing Problem

### 2.1.1. How Mobile IP Works

This section explains how Mobile IP works. The Mobile IP process has three main phases, which are discussed in the following sections.

- Agent Discovery - A Mobile Node discovers its Foreign and Home Agents during agent discovery.
- Registration - The Mobile Node registers its current location with the Foreign Agent and Home Agent during registration.

- Tunneling- A reciprocal tunnel is set up by the Home Agent to the care-of address (current location of the Mobile Node on the foreign network) to route packets to the Mobile Node as it roams.

### *Agent Discovery*

During the agent discovery phase, the Home Agent and Foreign Agent advertise their services on the network by using the ICMP Router Discovery Protocol (IRDP). The Mobile Node listens to these advertisements to determine if it is connected to its home network or foreign network.

The IRDP advertisements carry Mobile IP extensions that specify whether an agent is a Home Agent, Foreign Agent, or both; its care-of address; the types of services it will provide such as reverse tunneling and generic routing encapsulation (GRE); and the allowed registration lifetime or roaming period for visiting Mobile Nodes. Rather than waiting for agent advertisements, a Mobile Node can send out an agent solicitation. This solicitation forces any agents on the link to immediately send an agent advertisement.

If a Mobile Node determines that it is connected to a foreign network, it acquires a care-of address.

Two types of care-of addresses exist:

- Care-of address acquired from a Foreign Agent
- Colocated care-of address

A Foreign Agent care-of address is an IP address of a Foreign Agent that has an interface on the foreign network being visited by a Mobile Node. A Mobile Node that acquires this type of care-of address can share the address with other Mobile Nodes. A colocated care-of address is an IP address temporarily assigned to the interface of the Mobile Node itself. A colocated care-of address represents the current position of the Mobile Node on the foreign network and can be used by only one Mobile Node at a time.

When the Mobile Node hears a Foreign Agent advertisement and detects that it has moved outside of its home network, it begins registration.

### *Registration*

The Mobile Node is configured with the IP address and mobility security association (which includes the shared key) of its Home Agent. In addition, the Mobile Node is configured with either its home IP address, or another user identifier, such as a Network Access Identifier.

The Mobile Node uses this information along with the information that it learns from the Foreign Agent advertisements to form a Mobile IP registration request. It adds the registration request to its pending list and sends the registration request to its Home Agent either through the Foreign Agent or directly if it is using a colocated care-of address and is not required to register through the Foreign Agent. If the registration request is sent through the Foreign Agent, the Foreign Agent checks the validity of the registration request, which includes checking that the requested lifetime does not exceed its limitations, the requested tunnel encapsulation is available, and that reverse tunnel is supported. If the registration request is valid, the Foreign Agent adds the visiting Mobile Node to its pending list before relaying the request to the Home Agent. If the registration request is not valid, the Foreign Agent sends a registration reply with appropriate error code to the Mobile Node.

The Home Agent checks the validity of the registration request, which includes authentication of the Mobile Node. If the registration request is valid, the Home Agent creates a mobility binding (an association of the Mobile Node with its care-of address), a tunnel to the care-of address, and a routing entry for forwarding packets to the home address through the tunnel. The Home Agent then sends a registration reply to the Mobile Node through the Foreign Agent (if the registration request was received via the Foreign Agent) or directly to the Mobile Node. If the registration request is not valid, the Home Agent rejects the request by sending a registration reply with an appropriate error code.

The Foreign Agent checks the validity of the registration reply, including ensuring that an associated registration request exists in its pending list. If the registration reply is valid, the Foreign Agent adds the Mobile Node to its visitor list, establishes a tunnel to the Home Agent, and creates a routing entry for forwarding packets to the home address. It then relays the registration reply to the Mobile Node.

Finally, the Mobile Node checks the validity of the registration reply, which includes ensuring an associated request is in its pending list as well as proper authentication of the Home Agent. If the registration reply is not valid, the Mobile Node discards the reply. If a valid registration reply specifies that the registration is accepted, the Mobile Node is confirmed that the mobility agents are aware of its roaming. In the colocated care-of address case, it adds a tunnel to the Home Agent. Subsequently, it sends all packets to the Foreign Agent.

The Mobile Node reregisters before its registration lifetime expires. The Home Agent and Foreign Agent update their mobility binding and visitor entry, respectively, during reregistration. In the case where the registration is denied, the Mobile Node makes the necessary adjustments and attempts to register again. For example, if the registration is denied because of time mismatch and the Home Agent sends back its time stamp for synchronization, the Mobile Node adjusts the time stamp in future registration requests. Thus, a successful

Mobile IP registration sets up the routing mechanism for transporting packets to and from the Mobile Node as it roams.

### *Tunneling*

The Mobile Node sends packets using its home IP address, effectively maintaining the appearance that it is always on its home network. Even while the Mobile Node is roaming on foreign networks, its movements are transparent to correspondent nodes.

Data packets addressed to the Mobile Node are routed to its home network, where the Home Agent now intercepts and tunnels them to the care-of address toward the Mobile Node. Tunneling has two primary functions: encapsulation of the data packet to reach the tunnel endpoint, and decapsulation when the packet is delivered at that endpoint. The default tunnel mode is IP Encapsulation within IP Encapsulation. Optionally, GRE and minimal encapsulation within IP may be used.

Typically, the Mobile Node sends packets to the Foreign Agent, which routes them to their final destination, the Correspondent Node, as shown in Figure 2.2.

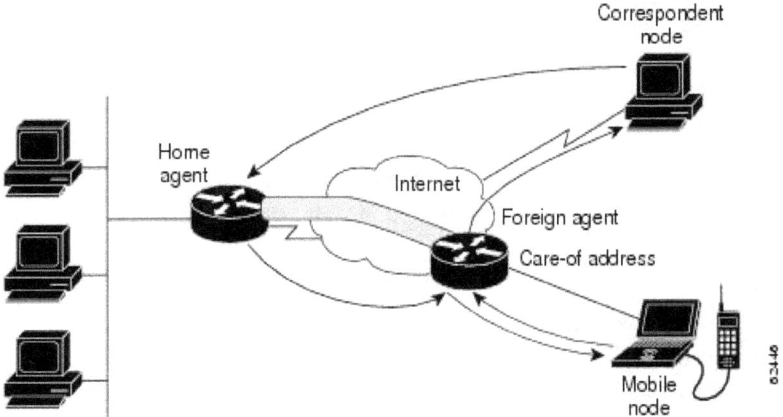


Fig. 2.2: Packet Forwarding

However, this data path is topologically incorrect because it does not reflect the true IP network source for the data-rather, it reflects the home network of the Mobile Node. Because the packets show the home network as their source inside a foreign network, an access control list on routers in the network called ingress filtering drops the packets instead of forwarding them. A feature called reverse tunneling solves this problem by having the Foreign Agent tunnel packets back to the Home Agent when it receives them from the Mobile Node. See Figure 2.3.

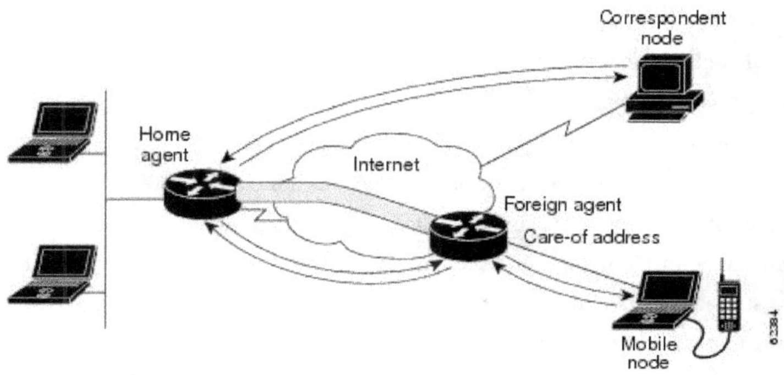


Fig. 2.3: Reverse Tunnel

Tunnel MTU discovery is a mechanism for a tunnel encapsulator such as the Home Agent to participate in path MTU discovery to avoid any packet fragmentation in the routing path between a Correspondent Node and Mobile Node. For packets destined to the Mobile Node, the Home Agent maintains the MTU of the tunnel to the care-of address and informs the Correspondent Node of the reduced packet size. This improves routing efficiency by avoiding fragmentation and reassembly at the tunnel endpoints to ensure that packets reach the Mobile Node.

## 2.2.    Features of Mobile IP

Mobile Internet Protocol (Mobile IP) was created in order to provide better mobile connectivity without interrupting computers that are already connected to a network. When mobile devices were introduced, there was no network technology in place for these devices to connect to the Internet. Mobile IP created a new subset of IP connectivity that worked within the already established system, keeping network engineers from having to scrap and reinvent the way Internet connection works.

- Roaming Connectivity - Mobile IP allows mobile devices to connect to the Internet when they are not at their home network. This lets laptops connect to hotspots and it lets phones connect through 3G and other Internet network sources. An IP address lets a network know where to send and receive information from on a network. Mobile IP uses an address that references its home network while finding a location on the new network. This keeps Mobile IP from knocking other computers off of a network, because each computer comes from a unique network and has a unique number.

- Compatibility - Mobile IP is compatible with most networks that offer the Internet. This include the 3G network used for mobile televisions; Internet hotspots found in cafes, airports and book stores; and all home network devices. Early attempts at Mobile IP would only work with certain routers or certain types of networks. Mobile IP today has no special requirements because the system is universal and fits within the original IP infrastructure.

- Tunneling and Reverse Tunneling - The method by which mobile IP receives information from a network is called tunneling. A network cannot directly send information to a mobile IP device. In order to get this information the mobile device must create an IP address within its new IP address. This allows the network to send information to the IP address through the "tunnel" of the two new IPs. Firewalls and routers can sometimes block tunneling by enabling what is called ingress filtering. Mobile IP also can use the process of reverse tunneling, which is a similar process that reverses the flow of information to achieve the same result as tunneling.

- Cordless - The greatest feature of Mobile IP is that there are no cords needed to complete the network connection. The standard IP required that networks be connected by a phone line or Ethernet cord. With Mobile IP, the device finds the network automatically and attempts to establish a connection. Some mobile capable devices like laptop computers have the ability to connect using the Mobile IP or using the standard IP with an Ethernet or phone cord.

- Security - Mobile IP should, as far as possible provide users with secure communication over the internet.

## 2.3. Key Mechanism in Mobile IP

Consists of 3 steps:
- Agent discovery,
- Registration, and
- Routing/Tunneling

### *Agent Discovery*

This consists of broadcast messages used by mobiles to detect that they have moved and are required to register with a new FA.

- FAs send agent advertisements
- MNs can solicit for agents if they have not heard an agent advertisement in awhile or use some other mechanism to obtain a COA or temp. IP address (e.g. DHCP).
- MNs know they are home when they recognize their HA.

### *Registration*

This used by a MN to inform the FA that it is visiting.

- The new care of address of the MN is sent to the HA.

- Registration expires, duration is negotiated during registration

- Mobile must re-register before it expires

- All registrations are authenticated

- The MN sends a registration request in to the FA which passes it along to the home agent. The HA responds to the FA which then informs the MN that all is in order and registration is complete.

### *Routing/Tunneling*

This consists of the delivery of the packets to the mobile node at its current care of address.

- Sender does not need to know that the destination is a MN.

- HA intercepts all packets for the MN and passes them along to MN using a tunnel.

- MN communicates directly with the CN.

- Referred to as Triangle Routing

## 2.4.    Overview of TCP/IP

The best place to start looking at TCP/IP is probably the name itself. TCP/IP in fact consists of dozens of different protocols, but only a few are the "main" protocols that define the core operation of the suite. Of these key protocols, two are usually considered the most important. The Internet Protocol (IP) is the primary OSI network layer (layer three) protocol that provides addressing, datagram routing and other functions in an internetwork. The Transmission Control Protocol (TCP) is the primary transport layer (layer four) protocol, and is responsible for connection establishment and management and reliable data transport between software processes on devices.

Due to the importance of these two protocols, their abbreviations have come to represent the entire suite: "TCP/IP". (In a moment we'll discover exactly the history of that name.) IP and TCP are important because many of TCP/IP's most critical functions are implemented at layers three and four. However, there is much more to TCP/IP than just TCP and IP. The protocol suite as a whole requires the work of many different protocols and technologies to make a functional network that can properly provide users with the applications they need.

TCP/IP uses its own four-layer architecture that corresponds roughly to the OSI Reference Model and provides a framework for the various protocols that comprise the suite. It also includes numerous high-level applications, some of which are well-known by Internet users who may not realize they are part of TCP/IP, such as HTTP (which runs the World Wide Web) and FTP. In the topics on TCP/IP architecture and protocols I provide an overview of most of the important TCP/IP protocols and how they fit together.

### 2.4.1. Early TCP/IP History

As I said earlier, the Internet is a primary reason why TCP/IP is what it is today. In fact, the Internet and TCP/IP are so closely related in their history that it is difficult to discuss one without also talking about the other. They were developed together, with TCP/IP providing the mechanism for implementing the Internet. TCP/IP has over the years continued to evolve to meet the needs of the Internet and also smaller, private networks that use the technology. I will provide a brief summary of the history of TCP/IP here; of course, whole books have been written on TCP/IP and Internet history, and this is a technical Guide and not a history book, so remember that this is just a quick look for sake of interest.

The TCP/IP protocols were initially developed as part of the research network developed by the United States Defense Advanced Research Projects Agency (DARPA or ARPA). Initially, this fledgling network, called the ARPAnet, was designed to use a number of protocols that had been adapted from existing technologies. However, they all had flaws or limitations, either in concept or in practical matters such as capacity, when used on the ARPAnet. The developers of the new network recognized that trying to use these existing protocols might eventually lead to problems as the ARPAnet scaled to a larger size and was adapted for newer uses and applications.

In 1973, development of a full-fledged system of internetworking protocols for the ARPAnet began. What many people don't realize is that in early versions of this technology, there was only one core protocol: TCP. And in fact, these letters didn't even stand for what they do today; they were for theTransmission Control Program. The first version of this predecessor of modern TCP was written in 1973, then revised and formally documented in RFC 675, Specification of Internet Transmission Control Program, December 1974.

Testing and development of TCP continued for several years. In March 1977, version 2 of TCP was documented. In August 1977, a significant turning point came in TCP/IP's development. Jon Postel, one of the most important pioneers of the Internet and TCP/IP, published a set of comments on the state of TCP. In that document (known as Internet Engineering Note number 2, or IEN 2), he provided what I consider superb evidence that reference models and layers aren't just for textbooks, and really are important to understand:

We are screwing up in our design of internet protocols by violating the principle of layering. Specifically we are trying to use TCP to do two things: serve as a host level end to end protocol, and to serve as an internet packaging and routing protocol. These two things should be provided in a layered and modular way. I suggest that a new distinct internetwork protocol is needed, and that TCP be used strictly as a host level end to end protocol.

Jon Postel, IEN 2, 1977

What Postel was essentially saying was that the version of TCP created in the mid-1970s was trying to do too much. Specifically, it was encompassing both layer three and layer four activities (in terms of OSI Reference Model layer numbers). His vision was prophetic, because we now know that having TCP handle all of these activities would have indeed led to problems down the road.

Postel's observation led to the creation of TCP/IP architecture, and the splitting of TCP into TCP at the transport layer and IP at the network layer; thus the name "TCP/IP". (As an aside, it's interesting, given this history, that sometimes the entire TCP/IP suite is called just "IP", even though TCP came first.) The process of dividing TCP into two portions began in version 3 of TCP, written in 1978. The first formal standard for the versions of IP and TCP used in modern networks (version 4) were created in 1980. This is why the first "real" version of IP is version 4 and not version 1. TCP/IP quickly became the standard protocol set for running the ARPAnet. In the 1980s, more and more machines and networks were connected to the evolving ARPAnet using TCP/IP protocols, and the TCP/IP Internet was born.

### 2.4.2. *Important Factors in the Success of TCP/IP*

TCP/IP was at one time just "one of many" different sets of protocols that could be used to provide network-layer and transport-layer functionality. Today there are still other options for internetworking protocol suites, but TCP/IP is the universally-accepted world-wide standard. Its growth in popularity has been due to a number of important factors. Some of these are historical, such as the fact that it is tied to the Internet as described above, while others are related to the characteristics of the protocol suite itself. Chief among these are the following:

- **Integrated Addressing System:** TCP/IP includes within it (as part of the Internet Protocol, primarily) a system for identifying and addressing devices on both small and large networks. The addressing system is designed to allow devices to be addressed regardless of the lower-level details of how each constituent network is constructed. Over time, the mechanisms for addressing in TCP/IP have improved, to meet the needs of growing networks, especially the Internet. The addressing system also includes a centralized administration capability for the Internet, to ensure that each device has a unique address.

- **Design For Routing:** Unlike some network-layer protocols, TCP/IP is specifically designed to facilitate the routing of information over a network of arbitrary complexity. In fact, TCP/IP is conceptually concerned more with the connection of networks, than with the connection of devices. TCP/IP routers enable data to be delivered between devices on different networks by moving it one step at a time from one network to the next. A number of support protocols are also included in TCP/IP to allow routers to exchange critical information and manage the efficient flow of information from one network to another.

- **Underlying Network Independence:** TCP/IP operates primarily at layers three and above, and includes provisions to allow it to function on almost any lower-layer technology, including LANs, wireless LANs and WANs of various sorts. This flexibility means that one can mix and match a variety of different underlying networks and connect them all using TCP/IP.

- **Scalability:** One of the most amazing characteristics of TCP/IP is how scalable its protocols have proven to be. Over the decades it has proven its mettle as the Internet has grown from a small network with just a few machines to a huge internetwork with millions of hosts. While some changes have been required periodically to support this growth, these changes have taken place as part of the TCP/IP development process, and the core of TCP/IP is basically the same as it was 25 years ago.

- **Open Standards and Development Process:** The TCP/IP standards are not proprietary, but open standards freely available to the public. Furthermore, the process used to develop TCP/IP standards is also completely open. TCP/IP standards and protocols are developed and modified using the unique, democratic "RFC" process, with all interested parties invited to participate. This ensures that anyone with an interest in the TCP/IP protocols is given a chance to provide input into their development, and also ensures the world-wide acceptance of the protocol suite.

## 2.5.  Architecture of TCP/IP

TCP/IP protocols map to a four-layer conceptual model known as the DARPA model, named after the U.S. government agency that initially developed TCP/IP. The four layers of the DARPA model are: Application, Transport, Internet, and Network Interface. Each layer in the DARPA model corresponds to one or more layers of the seven-layer Open Systems Interconnection (OSI) model.

Figure 2.4 shows the TCP/IP protocol architecture.

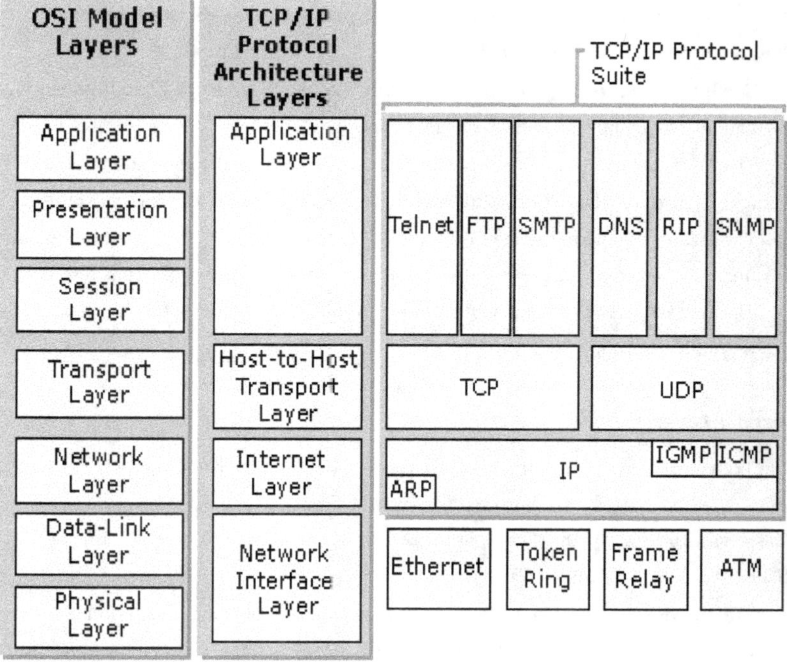


Fig. 2.4: TCP/IP Protocol Architecture

### *Network Interface Layer*

The Network Interface layer (also called the Network Access layer) is responsible for placing TCP/IP packets on the network medium and receiving TCP/IP packets off the network medium. TCP/IP was designed to be independent of the network access method, frame format, and medium. In this way, TCP/IP can be used to connect differing network types. These include LAN technologies such as Ethernet and Token Ring and WAN technologies such as X.25 and Frame Relay. Independence from any specific network technology gives TCP/IP the ability to be adapted to new technologies such as Asynchronous Transfer Mode (ATM).

The Network Interface layer encompasses the Data Link and Physical layers of the OSI model. Note that the Internet layer does not take advantage of sequencing and acknowledgment services that might be present in the Data-Link layer. An unreliable Network Interface layer is assumed, and reliable communications through session establishment and the sequencing and acknowledgment of packets is the responsibility of the Transport layer.

### *Internet Layer*

The Internet layer is responsible for addressing, packaging, and routing functions.

The core protocols of the Internet layer are IP, ARP, ICMP, and IGMP.

- The Internet Protocol (IP) is a routable protocol responsible for IP addressing, routing, and the fragmentation and reassembly of packets.
- The Address Resolution Protocol (ARP) is responsible for the resolution of the Internet layer address to the Network Interface layer address such as a hardware address.
- The Internet Control Message Protocol (ICMP) is responsible for providing diagnostic functions and reporting errors due to the unsuccessful delivery of IP packets.
- The Internet Group Management Protocol (IGMP) is responsible for the management of IP multicast groups.

The Internet layer is analogous to the Network layer of the OSI model.

### *Transport Layer*

The Transport layer (also known as the Host-to-Host Transport layer) is responsible for providing the Application layer with session and datagram communication services.

The core protocols of the Transport layer are Transmission Control Protocol (TCP) and the User Datagram Protocol (UDP).

- TCP provides a one-to-one, connection-oriented, reliable communications service. TCP is responsible for the establishment of a TCP connection, the sequencing and acknowledgment of packets sent, and the recovery of packets lost during transmission.
- UDP provides a one-to-one or one-to-many, connectionless, unreliable communications service. UDP is used when the amount of data to be transferred is small (such as the data that would fit into a single packet), when the overhead of establishing a TCP connection is not desired or when the applications or upper layer protocols provide reliable delivery.

The Transport layer encompasses the responsibilities of the OSI Transport layer and some of the responsibilities of the OSI Session layer.

### *Application Layer*

The Application layer provides applications the ability to access the services of the other layers and defines the protocols that applications use to exchange data. There are many Application layer protocols and new protocols are always being developed.

The most widely-known Application layer protocols are those used for the exchange of user information:

- The Hypertext Transfer Protocol (HTTP) is used to transfer files that make up the Web pages of the World Wide Web.
- The File Transfer Protocol (FTP) is used for interactive file transfer.
- The Simple Mail Transfer Protocol (SMTP) is used for the transfer of mail messages and attachments.
- Telnet, a terminal emulation protocol, is used for logging on remotely to network hosts.

Additionally, the following Application layer protocols help facilitate the use and management of TCP/IP networks:

- The Domain Name System (DNS) is used to resolve a host name to an IP address.

The Routing Information Protocol (RIP) is a routing protocol that routers use to exchange routing information on an IP internetwork.

- The Simple Network Management Protocol (SNMP) is used between a network management console and network devices (routers, bridges, intelligent hubs) to collect and exchange network management information.

## 2.6.    Adaptation of TCP Window

We have seen the importance of the concept of window size to TCP's sliding window mechanism. In a connection between a client and a server, the client tells the server the number of bytes it is willing to receive at one time from the server; this is the client's receive window, which becomes the server's send window. Likewise, the server tells the client how many bytes of data it is willing to take from the client at one time; this is the server'sreceive window and the client's send window.

The use of these windows is demonstrated in the topic discussing TCP's basic data transfer and acknowledgment mechanism. However, just as the example in that topic was simplified because I didn't show what happens with lost segments, there's another way that it doesn't reflect the real world conditions of an actual Internet: the send and receive window sizes never changed during the course of communication.

### *Impact of Buffer Management on TCP Window Size*

To understand why the window size may fluctuate, we need to understand what it represents. The simplest way of considering the window size is that it indicates the size of the device's receive buffer for the particular connection. That is, window size represents how much data a device can handle from its peer at one time before it is passed to the application process. Let's consider the aforementioned example. I said that the server's window size was 360. This means the server is willing to take no more than 360 bytes at a time from the client.

When the server receives data from the client, it places it into this buffer. The server must then do two distinct things with this data:

- **Acknowledgment:** The server must send an acknowledgment back to the client to indicate that the data was received.
- **Transfer:** The server must process the data, transferring it to the destination application process.

It is critically important that we differentiate between these two activities. Unfortunately, the TCP standards don't do a great job in this regard, which makes them very difficult to understand. The key point is that in the basic sliding windows system, data is acknowledged when received, but not necessarily immediately transferred out of the buffer. This means that is possible for the buffer to fill up with received data faster than the receiving TCP can empty it. When this occurs, the receiving device may need to adjust window size to prevent the buffer from being overloaded.

Since the window size can be used in this manner to manage the rate at which data flows between the devices at the ends of the connection, it is the method by which TCP implements flow control, one of the "classical" jobs of the transport layer. Flow control is vitally important to TCP, as it is the method by which devices communicate their status to each other. By reducing or increasing window size, the server and client each ensure that the other device sends data just as fast as the recipient can deal with it.

### *Reducing Send Window Size to Reduce the Rate Data is Sent*

Let's go back to our earlier example so I can hopefully explain better what I mean, but let's make a few changes. First, to keep things simple, let's just look at the transmissions made from the client to the server, not the server's replies (other than acknowledgments)—this is illustrated in.

As before, the client sends 140 bytes to the server. After sending the 140 bytes, the client has 220 bytes remaining in its usable window—360 in the send window less the 140 bytes it just sent.

Sometime later, the server receives the 140 bytes and puts them in the buffer. Now, in an "ideal world", the 140 bytes go into the buffer, are acknowledged and immediately removed from the buffer. Another way of thinking of this is that the buffer is of "infinite size" and can hold as much as the client can send.

The buffer's free space remains 360 bytes in size, so the same window size can be advertised back to the client. This was the "simplification" in the previous example.

## 2.7. Improvement in TCP Performance

### *TCP Slow Start*

The starting value of the cwnd window (the Initial Window, or IW) is set to that of the Sender Maximum Segment Size (SMSS) value. This SMSS value is based on the receiver's maximum segment size, obtained during the SYN handshake, the discovered path MTU (if used), the MTU of the sending interface, or, in the absence of other information, 536 bytes. The sender then enters a flow-control mode termed Slow Start.

The sender sends a single data segment, and because the window is now full, it then awaits the corresponding ACK. When the ACK is received, the sender increases its window by increasing the value ofcwnd by the value of SMSS. This then allows the sender to transmit two segments; at that point, the congestion window is again full, and the sender must await the corresponding ACKs for these segments. This algorithm continues by increasing the value of cwnd (and, correspondingly, opening the size of the congestion window) by one SMSS for every ACK received that acknowledges new data.

If the receiver is sending an ACK for every packet, the effect of this algorithm is that the data rate of the sender doubles every round-trip time interval. If the receiver supports delayed ACKs, the rate of increase will be slightly lower, but nevertheless the rate will increase by a minimum of one SMSS each round-trip time. Obviously, this cannot be sustained indefinitely. Either the value of cwnd will exceed the advertised receive window or the sender's window, or the capacity of the network will be exceeded, in which case packets will be lost.

There is another limit to the slow-start rate increase, maintained in a variable termed ssthresh, or Slow-Start Threshold. If the value ofcwnd increases past the value of ssthresh, the TCP flow-control mode is changed from Slow Start to congestion avoidance. Initially the value of ssthresh is set to the receiver's maximum window size.

However, when congestion is noted, ssthresh is set to half the current window size, providing TCP with a memory of the point where the onset of network congestion may be anticipated in future.

One aspect to highlight concerns the interaction of the slow-start algorithm with high-capacity long-delay networks, the so-called Long Fat Networks (or LFNs, pronounced "elephants"). The behavior of the slow-start algorithm is to send a single packet, await an ACK, then send two packets, and await the corresponding ACKs, and so on. The TCP activity on LFNs tends to cluster at each epoch of the round-trip time, with a quiet period that follows after the available window of data has been transmitted. The received ACKs arrive back at the sender with an inter-ACK spacing that is equivalent to the data rate of the bottleneck point on the network path. During Slow Start, the sender transmits at a rate equal to twice this bottleneck rate. The rate adaptation function that must occur within the network takes place in the router at the entrance to the bottleneck point. The sender's packets arrive at this router at twice the rate of egress from the router, and the router stores the overflow within its internal buffer. When this buffer overflows, packets will be dropped, and the slow-start phase is over. The important conclusion is that the sender will stop increasing its data rate when there is buffer exhaustion, a condition that may not be the same as reaching the true available data rate. If the router has a buffer capacity considerably less than the delay-bandwidth product of the egress circuit, the two values are certainly not the same.

In this case, the TCP slow-start algorithm will finish with a sending rate that is well below the actual available capacity. The efficient operation of TCP, particularly in LFNs, is critically reliant on adequately large buffers within the network routers.

Another aspect of Slow Start is the choice of a single segment as the initial sending window. Experimentation indicates that an initial value of up to four segments can allow for a more efficient session startup, particularly for those short-duration TCP sessions so prevalent with Web fetches [6]. Observation of Web traffic indicates an average Web data transfer of 17 segments. A slow start from one segment will take five RTT intervals to transfer this data, while using an initial value of four will reduce the transfer time to three RTT intervals. However, four segments may be too many when using low-speed links with limited buffers, so a more robust approach is to use an initial value of no more than two segments to commence Slow Start.

### *Packet Loss*

Slow Start attempts to start a TCP session at a rate the network can support and then continually increase the rate. How does TCP know when to stop this increase? This slow-start rate increase stops when the congestion window exceeds the receiver's advertised window, when the rate exceeds the remembered value of the onset of congestion as recorded in ssthresh, or when the rate is greater than the network can sustain. Addressing the last condition, how does a TCP sender know that it is sending at a rate greater than the network can sustain? The answer is that this is shown by data packets being dropped by the network. In this case, TCP has to undertake many functions:

- The packet loss has to be detected by the sender.
- The missing data has to be retransmitted.
- The sending data rate should be adjusted to reduce the probability of further packet loss.

TCP can detect packet loss in two ways. First, if a single packet is lost within a sequence of packets, the successful delivery packets following the lost packet will cause the receiver to generate a duplicate ACK for each successive packet. The reception of these duplicate ACKs is a signal of such packet loss. Second, if a packet is lost at the end of a sequence of sent packets, there are no following packets to generate duplicate ACKs. In this case, there are no corresponding ACKs for this packet, and the sender's retransmit timer will expire and the sender will assume packet loss.

A single duplicate ACK is not a reliable signal of packet loss. When a TCP receiver gets a data packet with an out-of-order TCP sequence value, the receiver must generate an immediate ACK of the highest in-order data byte received. This will be a duplicate of an earlier transmitted ACK. Where a single packet is lost from a sequence of packets, all subsequent packets will generate a duplicate ACK packet.

On the other hand, where a packet is rerouted with an additional incremental delay, the reordering of the packet stream at the receiver's end will generate a small number of duplicate ACKs, followed by an ACK of the entire data sequence, after the errant packet is received. The sender distinguishes between these cases by using three duplicate ACK packets as a signal of packet loss.

The third duplicate ACK triggers the sender to immediately send the segment referenced by the duplicate ACK value (fast retransmit) and commence a sequence termed Fast Recovery. In fast recovery, the value of ssthresh is set to half the current send window size (the send window is the amount of unacknowledged data outstanding). The congestion window, cwnd, is set three segments greater than ssthresh to allow for three segments already buffered at the receiver. If this allows additional data to be sent, then this is done. Each additional duplicate ACK inflates cwnd by a further segment size, allowing more data to be sent. When an ACK arrives that encompasses new data, the value of cwnd is set back to ssthresh, and TCP enters congestion-avoidance mode. Fast Recovery is intended to rapidly repair single packet loss, allowing the sender to continue to maintain the ACK-clocked data rate for new data while the packet loss repair is being undertaken. This is because there is still a sequence of ACKs arriving at the sender, so that the network is continuing to pass timing signals to the sender indicating the rate at which packets are arriving at the receiver. Only when the repair has been completed does the sender drop its window to the ssthresh value as part of the transition to congestion-avoidance mode [8].

The other signal of packet loss is a complete cessation of any ACK packets arriving to the sender. The sender cannot wait indefinitely for a delayed ACK, but must make the assumption at some point in time that the next unacknowledged data segment must be retransmitted. This is managed by the sender maintaining a Retransmission Timer. The maintenance of this timer has performance and efficiency implications. If the timer triggers too early, the sender will push duplicate data into the network unnecessarily. If the timer triggers too slowly, the sender will remain idle for too long, unnecessarily slowing down the flow of data. The TCP sender uses a timer to measure the elapsed time between sending a data segment and receiving the corresponding acknowledgment. Individual measurements of this time interval will exhibit significant variance, and implementations of TCP use a smoothing function when updating the retransmission timer of the flow with each measurement. The commonly used algorithm was originally described by Van Jacobson [9], modified so that the retransmission timer is set to the smoothed round-trip-time value, plus four times a smoothed mean deviation factor.

When the retransmission timer expires, the actions are similar to that of duplicate ACK packets, in that the sender must reduce its sending rate in response to congestion. The threshold value, ssthresh, is set to half of the current value of outstanding unacknowledged data, as in the duplicate ACK case. However, the sender cannot make any valid assumptions about the current state of the network, given that no useful information has been provided to the sender for more than one RTT interval. In this case, the sender closes the congestion window back to one segment, and restarts the flow in slow start -mode by sending a single segment. The difference from the initial slow start is that, in this case, the ssthresh value is set so that the sender will probe the congestion area more slowly using a linear sending rate increase when the congestion window reaches the remembered ssthresh value.

### *Congestion Avoidance*

Compared to Slow Start, congestion avoidance is a more tentative probing of the network to discover the point of threshold of packet loss. Where Slow Start uses an exponential increase in the sending rate to find a first-level approximation of the loss threshold, congestion avoidance uses a linear growth function.

When the value of cwnd is greater than ssthresh, the sender increments the value of cwnd by the value SMSS X SMSS/cwnd, in response to each received nonduplicate ACK [7], ensuring that the congestion window opens by one segment within each RTT time interval.

The congestion window continues to open in this fashion until packet loss occurs. If the packet loss is isolated to a single packet within a packet sequence, the resultant duplicate ACKs will trigger the sender to halve the sending rate and continue a linear growth of the congestion window from this new point, as described above in fast recovery.

Packet loss, as signaled by the triggering of the retransmission timer, causes the sender to recommence slow-start mode, following a timeout interval.

The inefficiency of this mode of performance is caused by the complete cessation of any form of flow signaling from the receiver to the sender. In the absence of any information, the sender can only assume that the network is heavily congested, and so must restart its probing of the network capacity with an initial congestion window of a single segment. This leads to the performance observation that any form of packet-drop management that tends to discard the trailing end of a sequence of data packets may cause significant TCP performance degradation, because such drop behavior forces the TCP session to continually time out and restart the flow from a single segment again.

## *Assisting TCP Performance Network-RED and ECN*

Although TCP is an end-to-end protocol, it is possible for the network to assist TCP in optimizing performance. One approach is to alter the queue behaviour of the network through the use of Random Early Detection (RED). RED permits a network router to discard a packet even when there is additional space in the queue. Although this may sound inefficient, the interaction between this early packet-drop behaviour and TCP is very effective.

RED uses a the weighted average queue length as the probability factor for packet drop. As the average queue length increases, the probability of a packet being dropped, rather than being queued, increases. As the queue length decreases, so does the packet-drop probability. Small packet bursts can pass through a RED filter relatively intact, while larger packet bursts will experience increasingly higher packet-discard rates. Sustained load will further increase the packet-discard rates. This implies that the TCP sessions with the largest open windows will have a higher probability of experiencing packet drop, causing a back-off in the window size.

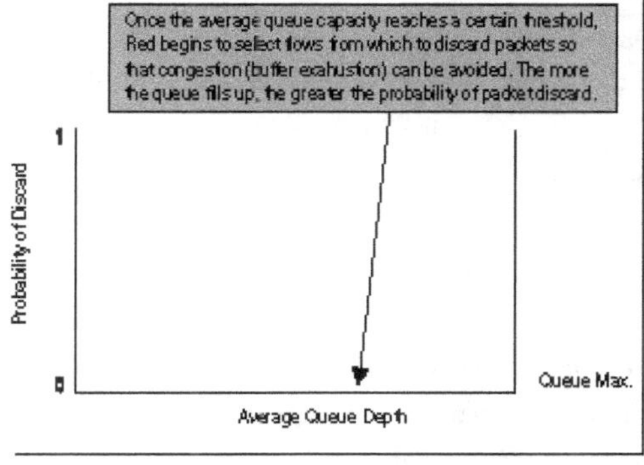


Fig. 2.5: Red Behavior

A major goal of RED is to avoid a situation in which all TCP flows experience congestion at the same time, all then back off and resume at the same rate, and tend to synchronize their behaviour . With RED, the larger bursting flows experience a higher probability of packet drop, while flows with smaller burst rates can continue without undue impact. RED is also intended to reduce the incidence of complete loss of ACK signals, leading to timeout and session restart in slow-start mode.

The intent is to signal the heaviest bursting TCP sessions the likelihood of pending queue saturation and tail drop before the onset of such a tail-drop congestion condition, allowing the TCP session to undertake a fast retransmit recovery under conditions of congestion avoidance. Another objective of RED is to allow the queue to operate efficiently, with the queue depth ranging across the entire queue size within a timescale of queue depth oscillation the same order as the average RTT of the traffic flows.

Behind RED is the observation that TCP sets very few assumptions about the networks over which it must operate, and that it cannot count on any consistent performance feedback signal being generated by the network.

As a minimal approach, TCP uses packet loss as its performance signal, interpreting small-scale packet-loss events as peak load congestion events and extended packet loss events as a sign of more critical congestion load. RED attempts to increase the number of small-scale congestion signals, and in so doing avoid long-period sustained congestion conditions.

It is not necessary for RED to discard the randomly selected packet. The intent of RED is to signal the sender that there is the potential for queue exhaustion, and that the sender should adapt to this condition.

An alternative mechanism is for the router experiencing the load to mark packets with an explicit Congestion Experienced (CE) bit flag, on the assumption that the sender will see and react to this flag setting in a manner comparable to its response to single packet drop [13] [14]. This mechanism, Explicit Congestion Notification (ECN), uses a 2-bit scheme, claiming bits 6 and 7 of the IP Version 4 Type-of-Service (ToS) field (or the two Currently Unused [CU] bits of the IP Differentiated Services field).

Bit 6 is set by the sender to indicate that it is an ECN-capable transport system (the ECT bit). Bit 7 is the CE bit, and is set by a router when the average queue length exceeds configured threshold levels.

The ECN algorithm is that an active router will perform RED, as described. After a packet has been selected, the router may mark the CE bit of the packet if the ECT bit is set; otherwise, it will discard the selected packet. (See Figure 2.6).

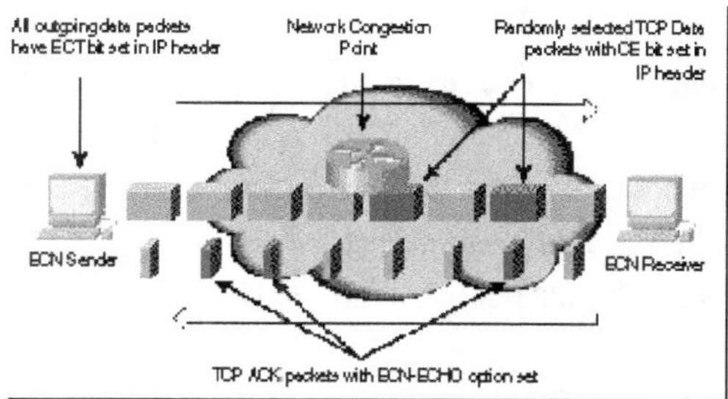


Fig. 2.6: Operation of Explicit Congestion Notification

The TCP interaction is slightly more involved. The initial TCP SYN handshake includes the addition of ECN-echo capability and Congestion Window Reduced (CWR) capability flags to allow each system to negotiate with its peer as to whether it will properly handle packets with the CE bit set during the data transfer. The sender sets the ECT bit in all packets sent. If the sender receives a TCP packet with the ECN-echo flag set in the TCP header, the sender will adjust its congestion window as if it had undergone fast recovery from a single lost packet.

The next sent packet will set the TCP CWR flag, to indicate to the receiver that it has reacted to the congestion. The additional caveat is that the sender will react in this way at most once every RTT interval. Further, TCP packets with the ECN-echo flag set will have no further effect on the sender within the same RTT interval. The receiver will set the ECN-echo flag in all packets when it receives a packet with the CE bit set. This will continue until it receives a packet with the CWR bit set, indicating that the sender has reacted to the congestion. The ECT flag is set only in packets that contain a data payload. TCP ACK packets that contain no data payload should be sent with the ECT bit clear.

The connection does not have to await the reception of three duplicate ACKs to detect the congestion condition. Instead, the receiver is notified of the incipient congestion condition through the explicit setting of a notification bit, which is in turn echoed back to the sender in the corresponding ACK. Simulations of ECN using a RED marking function indicate slightly superior throughput in comparison to configuring RED as a packet-discard function.

However, widespread deployment of ECN is not considered likely in the near future, at least in the context of Version 4 of IP. At this stage, there has been no explicit standardization of the field within the IPv4 header to carry this information, and the deployment base of IP is now so wide that any modifications to the semantics of fields in the IPv4 header would need to be very carefully considered to ensure that the changed field interpretation did not exercise some malformed behavior in older versions of the TCP stack or in older router software implementations.

ECN provides some level of performance improvement over a packet-drop RED scheme. With large bulk data transfers, the improvement is moderate, based on the difference between the packet retransmission and congestion-window adjustment of RED and the congestion-window adjustment of ECN. The most notable improvements indicated in ECN simulation experiments occur with short TCP transactions (commonly seen in Web transactions), where a RED packet drop of the initial data packet may cause a six-second retransmit delay. Comparatively, the ECN approach allows the transfer to proceed without this lengthy delay.

The major issue with ECN is the need to change the operation of both the routers and the TCP software stacks to accommodate the operation of ECN. While the ECN proposal is carefully constructed to allow an essentially uncoordinated introduction into the Internet without negative side effects, the effectiveness of ECN in improving overall network throughput will be apparent only after this approach has been widely adopted. As the Internet grows, its inertial mass generates a natural resistance to further technological change; therefore, it may be some years before ECN is widely adopted in both host software and Internet routing systems. RED, on the other hand, has had a more rapid introduction to the Internet, because it requires only a local modification to router behavior, and relies on existing TCP behavior to react to the packet drop.

### *Tuning TCP*

How can the host optimize its TCP stack for optimum performance? Many recommendations can be considered. The following suggestions are a combination of those measures that have been well studied and are known to improve TCP performance, and those that appear to be highly productive areas of further research and investigation [1].

- Use a good TCP protocol stack : Many of the performance pathologies that exist in the network today are not necessarily the byproduct of oversubscribed networks and consequent congestion. Many of these performance pathologies exist because of poor implementations of TCP flow-control algorithms; inadequate buffers within the receiver; poor (or no) use of path-MTU discovery; no support for fast-retransmit flow recovery, no use of window scaling and SACK, imprecise use of protocol-required timers, and very coarse-grained timers. It is unclear whether network ingress-imposed Quality-of-Service (QoS) structures will adequately compensate for such implementation deficiencies. The conclusion is that attempting to address the symptoms is not the same as curing the disease. A good protocol stack can produce even better results in the right environment.

- Implement a TCP Selective Acknowledgment (SACK) mechanism: SACK, combined with a selective repeat-transmission policy, can help overcome the limitation that traditional TCP experiences when a sender can learn only about a single lost packet per RTT.

- Implement larger buffers with TCP window-scaling options: The TCP flow algorithm attempts to work at a data rate that is the minimum of the delay-bandwidth product of the end-to-end network path and the available buffer space of the sender. Larger buffers at the sender and the receiver assist the sender in adapting more efficiently to a wider diversity of network paths by permitting a larger volume of traffic to be placed in flight across the end-to-end path.

- Support TCP ECN negotiation: ECN enables the host to be explicitly informed of conditions relating to the onset of congestion without having to infer such a condition from the reserve stream of ACK packets from the receiver. The host can react to such a condition promptly and effectively with a data flow-control response without having to invoke packet retransmission.

- Use a higher initial TCP slow-start rate than the current 1 MSS (Maximum Segment Size) per RTT. A size that seems feasible is an initial burst of 2 MSS segments. The assumption is that there will be adequate queuing capability to manage this initial packet burst; the provision to back off the send window to 1 MSS segment should remain intact to allow stable operation if the initial choice was too large for the path. A robust initial choice is two segments, although simulations have indicated that four initial segments is also highly effective in many situations.

- Use a host platform that has sufficient processor and memory capacity to drive the network. The highest-quality service network and optimally provisioned access circuits cannot compensate for a host system that does not have sufficient capacity to drive the service load. This is a condition that can be observed in large or very popular public Web servers, where the peak application load on the server drives the platform into a state of memory and processor exhaustion, even though the network itself has adequate resources to manage the traffic load.

All these actions have one thing in common: They can be deployed incrementally at the edge of the network and can be deployed individually. This allows end systems to obtain superior performance even in the absence of the network provider tuning the network's service response with various internal QoS mechanisms.

# Review Questions

## *Part A*

1. What is Mobile IP?
2. List the 2 agent discovery methods.
3. Define tunnelling.
4. What is TCP/IP?
5. What is the purpose of FTP?
6. List the layers present in the architecture of TCP/IP.
7. What is meant by slow start?
8. Give the functionality of Mobile IP.

## *Part B*

1. Explain about the key mechanism of Mobile IP.
2. Discuss about the architecture of TCP/IP with the neat diagram.
3. Explain about the adoption of TCP window.

# Unit-3

## Mobile Telecommunication System

### 3.1. Global System for Mobile Communication (GSM)

GSM is a globally accepted standard for digital cellular communications. GSM uses narrowband Time Division Multiple Access (TDMA) for providing voice and text based services over mobile phone networks.

#### 3.1.1. What is GSM?

- GSM stands for Global System for Mobile Communication. It is a digital cellular technology used for transmitting mobile voice and data services.

- The concept of GSM emerged from a cell-based mobile radio system at Bell Laboratories in the early 1970s.

- GSM is the name of a standardization group established in 1982 to create a common European mobile telephone standard.

- GSM is the most widely accepted standard in telecommunications and it is implemented globally.

- GSM is a circuit-switched system that divides each 200 kHz channel into eight 25 kHz time-slots. GSM operates on the mobile communication bands 900 MHz and 1800 MHz in most parts of the world. In the US, GSM operates in the bands 850 MHz and 1900 MHz.

- GSM owns a market share of more than 70 percent of the world's digital cellular subscribers.

- GSM makes use of narrowband Time Division Multiple Access (TDMA) technique for transmitting signals.

- GSM was developed using digital technology. It has an ability to carry 64 kbps to 120 Mbps of data rates.

- Presently GSM supports more than one billion mobile subscribers in more than 210 countries throughout the world.

- GSM provides basic to advanced voice and data services including roaming service. Roaming is the ability to use your GSM phone number in another GSM network.

- GSM digitizes and compresses data, then sends it down through a channel with two other streams of user data, each in its own timeslot.

### 3.1.2. *Why GSM?*

Listed below are the features of GSM that account for its popularity and wide acceptance.

- Improved spectrum efficiency
- International roaming
- Low-cost mobile sets and base stations (BSs)
- High-quality speech
- Compatibility with Integrated Services Digital Network (ISDN) and other telephone company services
- Support for new services

### 3.1.3. *GSM Services*

GSM provides three main categories of services. These are

- Bearer Services
- Teleservices
- Supplementary Services

The GSM system permits the integration of different voice and data services and the inter-working with existing networks. Services make a network flexible to users, i.e. they can choose one network over another. GSM has three different categories of services, bearer, tele and supplementary services And these are described in the following sections. Fig 3.1 shows a reference model for the GSM services.

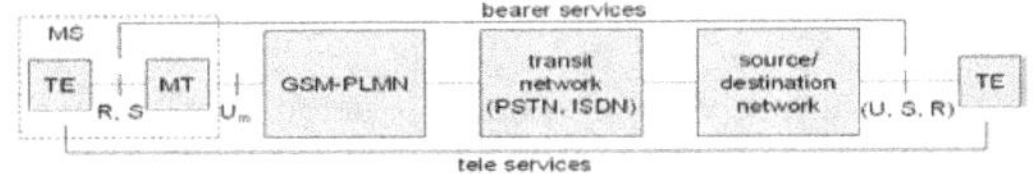


Fig. 3.1: Bearer and Teleservices Reference Model

A mobile station (MS) is connected to the GSM Public Land Mobile Network (PLMN) via the Um interface. This network is connected to the Transit network, e.g. Integrated Services Digital Network (ISDN) or the traditional Public Switched Telephone Network (PSTN) though there might also be an additional network, the Source/destination network, before another Terminal (TE) is connected. Bearer services now comprise all services that enable the transparent transmission of data between the interfaces to the network, i.e., S in the case of the MS, and a similar interface for the other terminal. In the original GSM model, bearer services are connection-orientated and circuit or packet switched and these services only need the lower three layers of the ISO/OSI reference model.

Within the mobile station (MS), the mobile terminal (MT) performs all the network specific tasks (such as TDMA, FDMA, coding, etc) and also offers the interface for data transmission (S) to the terminal (TE), which can then be independent of the network. Depending on the capabilities of the TE, more interfaces may be needed, such as R, according to ISDN reference model (Halsall, 1996). Tele services are application specific and may need all seven layers of the ISO/OSI reference model, these services are specified end-to-end, i.e. from one terminal (TE) to another terminal.

### *Bearer Services*

GSM specifies different mechanisms for data transmission for data transmission for the original GSM allowed for data rates up 9600 bit/s for non-voice services. Bearer services allow for both transparent and non-transparent, synchronous or asynchronous data transmission.

Transparent bearer services use only the functions of the physical layer (layer 1 ISO/OSI reference model) to transmit data; data transmission consequently has a constant delay and throughput, that is if no errors occur. The only mechanism of any use to try and increase the quality of the transmission is forward error correction (FEC).

Non-Transparent bearer services use protocols of the layers two and three to implement error correction and flow control. Non-transparent bearer services use the transparent bearer services, while adding a radio link protocol (RLP). This protocol uses mechanisms of high-level data link control (HDLC) (Halsall, 1996), and special selective-reject mechanisms to trigger retransmission of erroneous data. The achieved bit error rate is less than 10-7, but now throughput may vary, this depending on the transmission quality.

### *Teleservices*

GSM is mainly focused on voice tele services and these comprise of encrypted voice transmission, message services, and basic data communication with terminals as known from the PSTN or ISDN (e.g. fax). However as the main service is telephony, the primary goal of GSM was to provide high-quality digital voice transmission, offering at least the typical audio bandwidth of 3.1 kHz (which was what the old analogue systems offered). Special codecs (coder/decoder) are used for voice transmission. Different codecs are used for the transmission of data for communication with traditional computer modems, e.g. fax machines or the internet. Another tele service is the emergency number and this is the same number all over the GSM network in Europe and is also the same as the national emergency number. This is a mandatory service that all the network operators have to provide and is free of charge to the user. Another feature is that this service has the highest priority when connecting, possibly pre-empting other connections.

A useful additional service that is offered is the short message service (SMS), which is a simple text message transfer service, offering transmission of messages up to about 160 characters. SMS messages do not use the data channels, but instead uses the unused capacity in the signalling channel. The use of the signaling channel means that the user can send and receive SMS messages during a voice or data transmission.

### *Supplementary Services*

Further to bearer and tele services, GSM network operators can also offer supplementary services. These services offer enhancements to the standard telephony service and may differ from operator to operator, though typical services available to the user are caller location identifier (CLI), call forwarding, or redirection.

### *3.1.4.  GSM Architecture*

As with all telecommunications systems, GSM has a hierarchical and complex system architecture comprising of many entities, interfaces and acronyms Fig 3.2 shows a simplified overview of the GSM system as specified in the ETSI (TS 101.622). GSM systems consist of three subsystems,

- Radio Subsystem (RSS),
- Network and Switching Subsystem (NSS),
- Operation Subsystem (OSS).

Generally a GSM user will only notice a very small portion of the whole network, commonly the mobile stations (MS) and some antenna masts of the base transceiver stations (BTS).

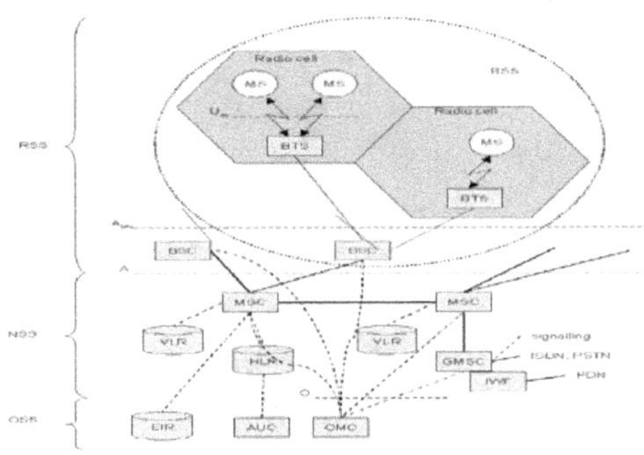

Fig. 3.2: Overview of GSM

### *Radio Subsystem (RSS)*

As suggested by the name, the radio subsystem is comprised of all the radio specific elements, i.e. the mobile stations (MS) and the base station subsystem (BSS).

**Base Station Subsystem (BSS):** A GSM network is made up of many BSSs, each one being controlled by a base station controller (BSC). The main function of the BSS is to maintain the radio connections to an MS, however, it does have several other functions such as the coding/decoding of voice, and rate adaptation to/from the wireless network part. As well as a BSC, the BSS contains several BTSs.

**Base Transceiver Station (BTS):** A BTS contains all the radio equipment (antennas, signal processing, amplifiers) necessary for radio transmission. A BTS can be used to form a radio cell, or if sectored antennas are used, several cells. The BTS is connected to the MS by the Um interface, and the BSC by the Abis interface. The Um interface comprises of all the mechanisms necessary for wireless transmission (TDMA, FDMA).

**Base Station Controller (BSC):** Basically, the BSC controls the BTS The functions of the BSC include reserving radio frequencies, handling handovers from one BTS to another and performing the paging of the MS. The BSC also multiplexes the radio channels onto the fixed network connections at the A interface.

**Mobile Station (MS) :** The MS is the user equipment which contains the software required for communication with the GSM network.

The MS consists of user independent hard/software and the subscriber identity module (SIM), which stores the user specific data. While an MS can be identified via the international mobile equipment identity (IMEI)

### *Network and Switching Subsystem (NSS)*

At the centre of any GSM system there is the network and switching subsystem (NSS) that connects the GSM network with the public land network (i.e. a PSTN), performs the handovers between BSS's, comprises functions for worldwide localization of users and supports charging, accounting and roaming of users between different networks and in different countries.
The NSS is comprised of the following switches and databases:

**Mobile services switching centre (MSC):** High-performance digital ISDN switches, that set up the connections between other MSC's and the BSC's, using the A interface. Hence the MSC's are the backbone of any GSM network. Normally one MSC will manage many BSC's in a geographical area. Some MSC's are gateway MSC (GMSC) that provide connections to other fixed networks (e.g. PSTN).

**Home Location Register (HLR):** The most important database in a GSM network is the HLR as it stores all the relevant information about the users. Information such as the mobile station ISDN number (MSISDN), services subscribed to, and the authentication key Ki. Furthermore the HLR stores dynamic information like the LA (Location Area) of the MS. As the MS moves geographically around the GSM network, the HLR stores the location of the MS from the LA. This information is used to localize the user within the worldwide GSM network. All of these user specific information elements only exist once for each user in a single HLR. The HLR also supports charging and accounting.

**Visitor Location Register (VLR):** The VLR associated to each MSC is a very dynamic database which stores all important information needed for the MS users currently in the LA that is associated to the MSC. If a new MS comes into the LA then the VLR is responsible for it. The VLR copies all the relevant information for the MS from the HLR. The structure of the VLR and HLR avoids frequent updates and long-distance signalling of user information.

### *Operation Subsystem (OSS)*

The GSM system is broken up in to three parts, the first two parts have already been discussed, the third part of the GSM system is the operational subsystem (OSS).

The OSS contains all the functions necessary for network operation and maintenance. The OSS possesses network entities of its own and accesses other entities via SS7 signaling.
The following section describes the entities:

Operation and Maintenance Centre (OMC): The OMC monitors and controls all other GSM network entities via the O interface (SS7 with X.25), typically the OMC functions are Traffic Monitoring, Status reports of the network entities, subscribers and security management, or accounting and billing.

Authentication Centre (AuC): The Radio Air interface and the MS's are particularly vulnerable, therefore a separate AuC has been defined to protect user identity and data transmission. The AuC contains the algorithms for authentication, the keys for encryption and generates the values needed for user authentication for the HLR.

Equipment Identity Register (EIR): EIR is a database for all IMEIs that stores all the device identifications registered for the GSM network. As MSs are mobile they can be stolen easily. If a user has a valid SIM of their own, then they can use any stolen MS.

Hence the EIR has a 'black list' of stolen or locked devices so the MS on this list is useless as soon as the owner of the MS has reported it as stolen. Furthermore the EIR holds a list of valid IMEIs, and a list of malfunctioning devices.

### *3.1.5.  GSM Security*

The GSM system has several security services for security, these security services use confidential information that is stored in the AuC and in the customers SIM (Subscriber Identity Module) chip. The SIM chip may be plugged into any MS, however for the SIM chip to allow access to the MS the user must enter a PIN (Personal Identification Number), the SIM chip contain personal, secret data. The following are the security services offered by GSM:

- **Authentication and Access Control:** For any MS to be used on the GSM network a number of events have to take place, the first event includes the authentication of a valid user for the SIM, the user enters their secret PIN to access the SIM.
- **Confidentiality:** All data that is related to the user is encrypted, after authentication the BTS and MS apply encryption to data, voice and signalling. This confidentiality only exist between the BTS and MS, however it does not exist end-to-end or within the whole fixed GSM/telephone network.
- **Anonymity:** The GSM system also provides a level of anonymity, all of the data is encrypted before transmission, and user identifiers that would show the identity of a user are not used over the air. Instead the GSM system uses a temporary identifier (TMSI), this is newly assigned by the VLR after each location update. Furthermore the VLR can change the TMSI at any time.

## 3.2.   General Packet Radio Service (GPRS)

### *What is GPRS?*

It is a packet oriented mobile data service on the 2G and 3G cellular communication system's global system for mobile communications (GSM). GPRS was originally standardized by European Telecommunications Standards Institute (ETSI) in response to the earlier CDPD and i-mode packet-switched cellular technologies. It is now maintained by the 3rd Generation Partnership Project (3GPP). GPRS usage is typically charged based on volume of data transferred, contrasting with circuit switched data, which is usually billed per minute of connection time. Usage above the bundle cap is charged per megabyte, speed limited, or disallowed.

### *3.2.1.  GPRS Services*

GPRS offers end-to-end packet switched data transfer services which can be catergorized into the following two types:

- Point–to–Point Services(PTP): This is between 2 users and can either be connectionless or connection oriented.

- Point–to–Multipoint Services (PTM): This is data transfer between 1 user to multiple users. Again this has 2 types

  - Multicast PTM –Data packets are broadcasted in certain areas.

  - Group Call PTM –Data packets are addressed to a group of users.

### 3.2.2. GPRS Architecture

GPRS architecture works on the same procedure like GSM network, but, has additional entities that allow packet data transmission. This data network overlaps a second-generation GSM network providing packet data transport at the rates from 9.6 to 171 kbps. Along with the packet data transport the GSM network accommodates multiple users to share the same air interface resources concurrently. Fig 3.3 is the GPRS Architecture diagram:

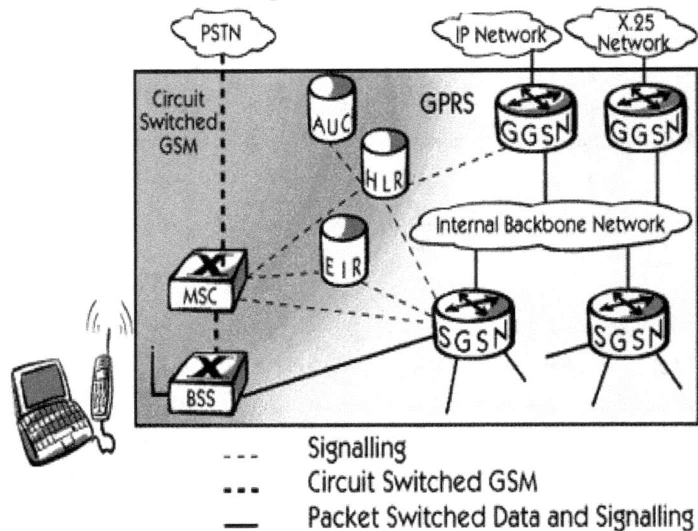


Fig. 3.3: GPRS Architecture

GPRS attempts to reuse the existing GSM network elements as much as possible, but to effectively build a packet-based mobile cellular network, some new network elements, interfaces, and protocols for handling packet traffic are required. Therefore, GPRS requires modifications to numerous GSM network elements as summarized below:

| GSM Network Element | Modification or Upgrade Required for GPRS. |
|---|---|
| Mobile Station (MS) | New Mobile Station is required to access GPRS services. These new terminals will be backward compatible with GSM for voice calls. |
| BTS | A software upgrade is required in the existing Base Transceiver Station(BTS). |
| BSC | The Base Station Controller (BSC) requires a software upgrade and the installation of new hardware called the packet control unit (PCU). The PCU directs the data traffic to the GPRS network and can be a separate hardware element associated with the BSC. |
| GPRS Support Nodes (GSNs) | The deployment of GPRS requires the installation of new core network elements called the serving GPRS support node (SGSN) and gateway GPRS support node (GGSN). |
| Databases (HLR, VLR, etc.) | All the databases involved in the network will require software upgrades to handle the new call models and functions introduced by GPRS. |

### *GPRS Mobile Stations*

New Mobile Stations (MS) are required to use GPRS services because existing GSM phones do not handle the enhanced air interface or packet data.

A variety of MS can exist, including a high-speed version of current phones to support high-speed data access, a new PDA device with an embedded GSM phone, and PC cards for laptop computers. These mobile stations are backward compatible for making voice calls using GSM.

### *GPRS Base Station Subsystem*

Each BSC requires the installation of one or more Packet Control Units (PCUs) and a software upgrade. The PCU provides a physical and logical data interface to the Base Station Subsystem (BSS) for packet data traffic. The BTS can also require a software upgrade but typically does not require hardware enhancements.

When either voice or data traffic is originated at the subscriber mobile, it is transported over the air interface to the BTS, and from the BTS to the BSC in the same way as a standard GSM call. However, at the output of the BSC, the traffic is separated; voice is sent to the Mobile Switching Center (MSC) per standard GSM, and data is sent to a new device called the SGSN via the PCU over a Frame Relay interface.

### *GPRS Support Nodes*

Following two new components, called Gateway GPRS Support Nodes (GSNs) and, Serving GPRS Support Node (SGSN) are added:

### *Gateway GPRS Support Node (GGSN)*

The Gateway GPRS Support Node acts as an interface and a router to external networks. It contains routing information for GPRS mobiles, which is used to tunnel packets through the IP based internal backbone to the correct Serving GPRS Support Node. The GGSN also collects charging information connected to the use of the external data networks and can act as a packet filter for incoming traffic.

### Serving GPRS Support Node (SGSN)

The Serving GPRS Support Node is responsible for authentication of GPRS mobiles, registration of mobiles in the network, mobility management, and collecting information on charging for the use of the air interface.

### Internal Backbone

The internal backbone is an IP based network used to carry packets between different GSNs. Tunnelling is used between SGSNs and GGSNs, so the internal backbone does not need any information about domains outside the GPRS network. Signalling from a GSN to a MSC, HLR or EIR is done using SS7.

### Routing Area

GPRS introduces the concept of a Routing Area. This concept is similar to Location Area in GSM, except that it generally contains fewer cells. Because routing areas are smaller than location areas, less radio resources are used While broadcasting a page message.

## 3.3.  Universal Mobile Telecommunications System (UMTS)

The *Universal Mobile Telecommunications System (UMTS)* is a third generation mobile cellular system for networks based on the GSM standard. Developed and maintained by the 3GPP (3rd Generation Partnership Project), UMTS is a component of the International Telecommunications Union IMT-2000 standard set and compares with the CDMA2000 standard set for networks based on the competing cdma One technology. UMTS uses wideband code division multiple access(W-CDMA) radio access technology to offer greater spectral efficiency and bandwidth to mobile network operators. UMTS specifies a complete network system, which includes the radio access network (UMTS Terrestrial Radio Access Network, or UTRAN), the core network(Mobile Application Part, or MAP) and the authentication of users via SIM (subscriber identity module) cards. The technology described in UMTS is sometimes also referred to as Freedom of Mobile Multimedia Access (FOMA)[1] or 3GSM.

### 3.3.1.  UMTS Architecture

The UMTS 3G architecture is required to provide a greater level of performance to that of the original GSM network. However as many networks had migrated through the use of GPRS and EDGE, they already had the ability to carry data. Accordingly many of the elements required for the WCDMA/UMTS network architecture were seen as a migration. This considerably reduced the cost of implementing the UMTS network as many elements were in place or needed upgrading. With one of the major aims of UMTS being to be able to carry data, the UMTS network architecture was designed to enable a considerable improvement in data performance over that provided for GSM. The UMTS network architecture(Fig 3.4) can be divided into three main elements:

- **User Equipment (UE):**  The User Equipment or UE is the name given to what was previous termed the mobile, or cellphone. The new name was chosen because the considerably greater functionality that the UE could have. It could also be anything between a mobile phone used for talking to a data terminal attached to a computer with no voice capability.

- **Radio Network Subsystem (RNS):**  The RNS also known as the UMTS Radio Access Network, UTRAN, is the equivalent of the previous Base Station Subsystem or BSS in GSM. It provides and manages the air interface for the overall network.

- **Core Network:**  The core network provides all the central processing and management for the system. It is the equivalent of the GSM Network Switching Subsystem or NSS.

The core network is then the overall entity that interfaces to external networks including the public phone network and other cellular telecommunications networks.

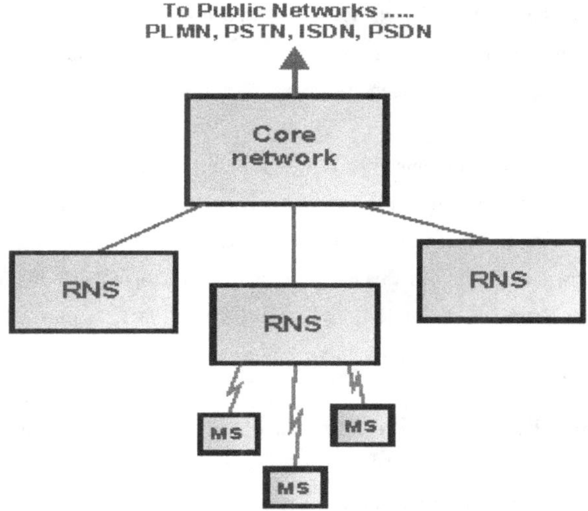


Fig. 3.4: UMTS Network Architecture Overview

### *User Equipment, UE*

The USER Equipment or UE is a major element of the overall 3G UMTS network architecture.

It forms the final interface with the user. In view of the far greater number of applications and facilities that it can perform, the decision was made to call it a user equipment rather than a mobile.

However it is essentially the handset (in the broadest terminology), although having access to much higher speed data communications, it can be much more versatile, containing many more applications.

It consists of a variety of different elements including RF circuitry, processing, antenna, battery, etc.

There are a number of elements within the UE that can be described separately:

- **UE RF Circuitry:**  The RF areas handle all elements of the signal, both for the receiver and for the transmitter. One of the major challenges for the RF power amplifier was to reduce the power consumption. The form of modulation used for W-CDMA requires the use of a linear amplifier. These inherently take more current than non linear amplifiers which can be used for the form of modulation used on GSM. Accordingly to maintain battery life, measures were introduced into many of the designs to ensure the optimum efficiency.

- **Baseband Processing:**  The base-band signal processing consists mainly of digital circuitry. This is considerably more complicated than that used in phones for previous generations. Again this has been optimised to reduce the current consumption as far as possible.

- **Battery:**  While current consumption has been minimised as far as possible within the circuitry of the phone, there has been an increase in current drain on the battery. With users expecting the same lifetime between charging batteries as experienced on the previous generation phones, this has necessitated the use of new and improved battery technology. Now Lithium Ion (Li-ion) batteries are used. These phones to remain small and relatively light while still retaining or even improving the overall life between charges.

- **Universal Subscriber Identity Module, USIM:**  The UE also contains a SIM card, although in the case of UMTS it is termed a USIM (Universal Subscriber Identity Module). This is a more advanced version of the SIM card used in GSM and other systems, but embodies the same types of information. It contains the International

Mobile Subscriber Identity number (IMSI) as well as the Mobile Station International ISDN Number (MSISDN). Other information that the USIM holds includes the preferred language to enable the correct language information to be displayed, especially when roaming, and a list of preferred and prohibited Public Land Mobile Networks (PLMN). The USIM also contains a short message storage area that allows messages to stay with the user even when the phone is changed. Similarly "phone book" numbers and call information of the numbers of incoming and outgoing calls are stored.

The UE can take a variety of forms, although the most common format is still a version of a "mobile phone" although having many data capabilities. Other broadband dongles are also being widely used.

### *3G UMTS Radio Network Subsystem*

- This is the section of the 3G UMTS / WCDMA network that interfaces to both the UE and the core network.
- The overall radio access network, i.e. collectively all the Radio Network Subsystem is known as the UTRAN UMTS Radio Access Network.
- The radio network subsystem is also known as the UMTS Radio Access Network or UTRAN.
- Read more about the **UMTS Radio Access Network.**

### *3G UMTS Core Network*

The 3G UMTS core network architecture is shown in fig 3.5 is a migration of that used for GSM with further elements overlaid to enable the additional functionality demanded by UMTS.

In view of the different ways in which data may be carried, the UMTS core network may be split into two different areas:

- **Circuit Switched Elements:**  These elements are primarily based on the GSM network entities and carry data in a circuit switched manner, i.e. a permanent channel for the duration of the call.
- **Packet Switched Elements:**  These network entities are designed to carry packet data. This enables much higher network usage as the capacity can be shared and data is carried as packets which are routed according to their destination.

Some network elements, particularly those that are associated with registration are shared by both domains and operate in the same way that they did with GSM.

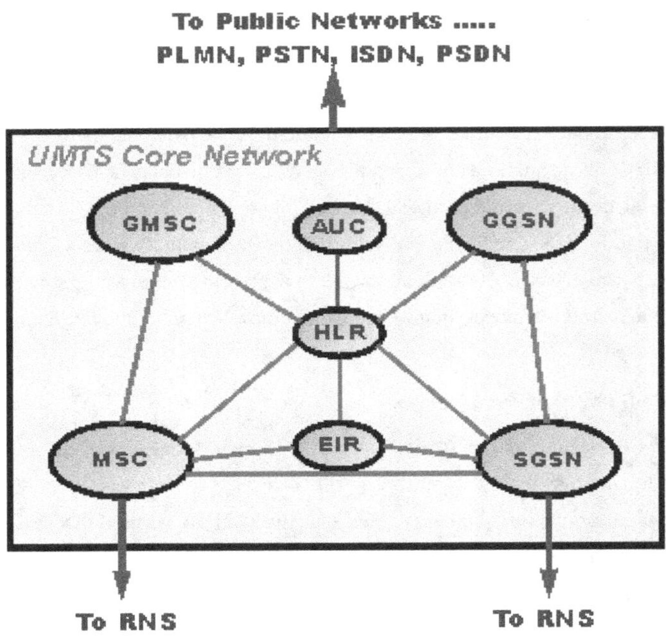


Fig. 3.5: UMTS Core Network

**Circuit Switched Elements:** The circuit switched elements of the UMTS core network architecture include the following network entities:

- **Mobile Switching Centre (MSC):**  This is essentially the same as that within GSM, and it manages the circuit switched calls under way.

- **Gateway MSC (GMSC):**  This is effectively the interface to the external networks.

- **Packet Switched Elements:** The packet switched elements of the 3G UMTS core network architecture include the following network entities:

- **Serving GPRS Support Node (SGSN):**  As the name implies, this entity was first developed when GPRS was introduced, and its use has been carried over into the UMTS network architecture.

- The SGSN provides a number of functions within the UMTS network architecture.

    - Mobility management  When a UE attaches to the Packet Switched domain of the UMTS Core Network, the SGSN generates MM information based on the mobile's current location.

- Session management:  The SGSN manages the data sessions providing the required quality of service and also managing what are termed the PDP (Packet data Protocol) contexts, i.e. the pipes over which the data is sent.

- Interaction with other areas of the network:  The SGSN is able to manage its elements within the network only by communicating with other areas of the network, e.g. MSC and other circuit switched areas.

- Billing:  The SGSN is also responsible billing. It achieves this by monitoring the flow of user data across the GPRS network. CDRs (Call Detail Records) are generated by the SGSN before being transferred to the charging entities (Charging Gateway Function, CGF).

- **Gateway GPRS Support Node (GGSN):**  Like the SGSN, this entity was also first introduced into the GPRS network. The Gateway GPRS Support Node (GGSN) is the central element within the UMTS packet switched network. It handles inter-working between the UMTS packet switched network and external packet switched networks, and can be considered as a very sophisticated router. In operation, when the GGSN receives data addressed to a specific user, it checks if the user is active and then forwards the data to the SGSN serving the particular UE.

- **Shared Elements:** The shared elements of the 3G UMTS core network architecture include the following network entities:

  - **Home location register (HLR):**  This database contains all the administrative information about each subscriber along with their last known location. In this way, the UMTS network is able to route calls to the relevant RNC / Node B. When a user switches on their UE, it registers with the network and from this it is possible to determine which Node B it communicates with so that incoming calls can be routed appropriately. Even when the UE is not active (but switched on) it re-registers periodically to ensure that the network (HLR) is aware of its latest position with their current or last known location on the network.

  - **Equipment identity register (EIR):**  The EIR is the entity that decides whether a given UE equipment may be allowed onto the network. Each UE equipment has a number known as the International Mobile Equipment Identity. This number, as mentioned above, is installed in the equipment and is checked by the network during registration.

  - **Authentication centre (AuC) :**  The AuC is a protected database that contains the secret key also contained in the user's USIM card.

# Review Questions

## *Part A*

1. What is GSM?
2. List the services provided by GSM.
3. Give the sub categories of GSM.
4. Differentiate HLR and VLR.
5. What is EIR?
6. Is GSM secured? Justify.
7. What is GPRS?
8. List the services provided by GPRS.
9. What is UMTS?
10. What is meant by RNS?

## *Part B*

1. With the neat diagram explain about GSM Architecture.
2. Briefly discuss about the service and architecture of GPRS with a diagram.
3. What is UMTS? Explain the architecture of UMTS.

# UNIT-4

## MOBILE AD-HOC NETWORKS

## 4.1.  Ad-Hoc Basic Concepts

- Wireless networks are vital role played by networking infrastructures such as hubs, routers, and base stations in their operation.

- However, such networking infrastructure may not be available in many situations such as disaster-hit locality or a remove location as we have already pointed out.

- Mobile IP requires, e.g., a home agent, tunnels, and default routers. DHCP requires servers and broadcast capabilities of the medium reaching all participants or relays to servers.

- Cellular phone networks require base stations, infrastructure networks etc.

- However, there may be several situations where users of a network cannot rely on an infrastructure, it is too expensive, or there is none at all.

- In these situations mobile ad-hoc networks are the only choice.

- It is important to note that this section focuses on so-called multi-hop ad-hoc networks when describing adhoc networking.

- The ad-hoc setting up of a connection with an infrastructure is not the main issue here.

- These networks should be mobile and use wireless communications.

- Examples for the use of such mobile, wireless, multi-hop ad-hoc networks, which are only called ad-hoc networks here for simplicity are:

  1. **Instant infrastructure:** Unplanned meetings, spontaneous interpersonal communications etc. cannot rely on any infrastructure. Infrastructures need planning and administration. It would take too long to set up this kind of infrastructure; therefore, ad-hoc connectivity has to be set up.

  2. **Disaster relief:** Infrastructures typically break down in disaster areas. Hurricanes cut phone and power lines, floods destroy base stations, fires burn servers. Emergency teams can only rely on an infrastructure they can set up themselves. No forward planning can be done, and the set-up must be extremely fast and reliable. The same applies to many military activities, which is, to be honest, one of the major driving forces behind mobile ad-hoc networking research.

  3. **Remote areas:** Even if infrastructures could be planned ahead, it is sometimes too expensive to set up an infrastructure in sparsely populated areas. Depending

on the communication pattern, ad-hoc networks or satellite infrastructures can be a solution.

4. **Effectiveness:** Services provided by existing infrastructures might be too expensive for certain applications. If, for example, only connection oriented cellular networks exist, but an application sends only small status information every other minute, a cheaper ad-hoc packet-oriented network might be a better solution. Registration procedures might take too long, and communication overheads might be too high with existing networks. Application-tailored ad-hoc networks can offer a better solution.

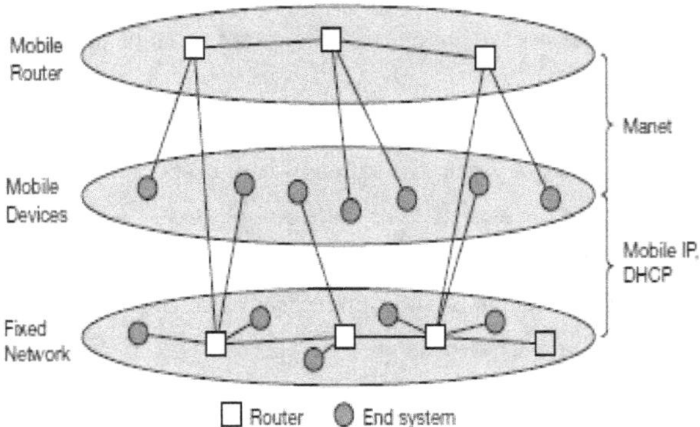



Fig. 4.1: MANETs and Mobile IP

## 4.2.  Characteristics

These characteristics trying to improvise new network protocols or extend the traditional network protocols for use in a MANET. A few of important characteristics of MANET are described below:

### i.  *Lack of Fixed Infrastructure*

- Lack of any specific networking infrastructure is possibly the most distinguishing characteristics of a MANET.
- In the absence of any fixed networking infrastructure, a pair of nodes can either communicate directly when they are in the transmission range of each other.
- Based on these characteristics cellular networks and wireless LANs cannot be considered to be MANETs.

## ii. *Dynamics Topologies*

- It is allowed to move arbitrarily, the network topology can change unpredictably.
- The rate of topology change depends on the speed of movement of the mobile devices.
- The speed of movement of a mobile device can vary greatly with the time of the day and specific MANET application being considered.

## iii. *Bandwidth Constrained, Variable Capacity Links*

- Wireless links have significantly lower capacity than their wired counterparts.
- Factors such as fading, noise, and interference can change the available bandwidth of a wireless link arbitrarily with the time.

## iv. *Energy Constrained Operation*

- The nodes in a MANET rely on battery power.
- These batteries are small and can store very limited amounts of energy.
- On the other hand, transmissions and processing required during routing involve expenditure of substantial amount of energy causing the batteries to get rapidly drained out, unless the routing protocol is carefully designed.

## v. *Increased Vulnerability*

- MANETs are prone to many new types of security threats that do not exist in the case of their wired counterparts.
- Many of these threats arise due to the underlying wireless transmissions and the deployment of collaborative routing techniques.
- Further, there are increased possibilities of eavesdropping, spoofing, denial of service attacks in these networks.

## *Other Characteristics*

- It include a distributed peer to peer mode of operation, multi-hop routing, and relatively frequent changes to the concentration of nodes over any specific area.

## 4.3.  Applications

- A MANET can be set up quickly since no fixed infrastructures need to be deployed.
- Thus, in any situation where fixed infrastructure becomes difficult to be set up because of security, cost, inaccessibility of the terrain, or safety-related reasons, ad-hoc networks become the preferred choice.

- A few example applications are defence related operations and disaster management applications.

## 1. *Communication among Portable Computers*

- Miniaturization has allowed the development of many types of portables and computerized equipment, which have become very popular.
- Many of these portables work meaningfully when connected to some network, possibly a LAN or Internet.
- For this, portables are typically required to be within the range of some wireless hub.
- However, dramatically reduce the flexibility and the mobility of the devices.

## 2. *Environmental Monitoring*

- It is collection of the various types of data about the environment in which they are deployed.
- Continuous data collection from remote locations is considered important for several applications such as environmental management, security monitoring, road traffic monitoring and management etc.,
- Miniaturized sensors have proved to be an effective means of gathering environmental information such as   rainfall, humidity, presence of certain animals etc.,

## 3. *Military*

- The present day military equipment have become quite sophisticated, have many automated parts and contain one or more computers.
- Scope of setting up an ad-hoc network consisting of various military equipment deployed in a frontline battle field.
- Ad-hoc networking of these equipment can allow a military setup to take advantage of an information network among the soldiers, vehicles, and military information headquarters.

## 4. *Emergency Application*

- Ad-hoc networks do not require any pre-existing infrastructure.
- It can be deployed easily and rapidly in emergency situations such as a search and rescue operation after a natural disaster, and for applications such as policing and fire fighting.

## 4.4.    Design Issues

We point out below a few important issues that are relevant to the design of suitable MANET protocols.

### 1.   Network Size and Node Density

- Network size and node density are the two important parameters of a MANET.
- Network size refers to the geographical coverage area of the network.
- Network density refers to the number of nodes present per unit geographical area.

### 2.   Connectivity

- It is usually refers to the number of neighbours.
- Here a neighbour of a node is one that is in its transmission range.
- The term connectivity is also sometimes used to refer to a link between the two nodes.
- The term link capacity denotes the bandwidth of the link.
- In a MANET, both the number of neighbouring nodes and the capacities of the links to different neighbours may vary significantly.

### 3.   Network Topology

- It denotes the connectivity among the various nodes of the network.
- Mobility of the nodes affects the network topology.
- Due to node mobility, new links can form and some links may get dissolved.
- Other than mobility, nodes can become inoperative due to discharged batteries or hardware failures and thereby cause changes to the topology.

### 4.   User Traffic

- It is based on the anticipated node density, average rate of node movements and the expected traffic.
- A network protocol should leverage the characteristics of specific traffic types that are expected to improve its performance.
- The common traffic types are the following
    1. Bursty traffic
    2. Large packets sent periodically
    3. Combination of the above two types of traffic

### 5. *Operational Environment*

- Operational Environment of a mobile network is usually urban, rural, and maritime.
- It supports the Line Of Sight (LOS) Communication.
- It requires different designs of mobile networks to suit an Operational Environment.

### 6. *Energy Constraint*

- It has no fixed infrastructure exists in a MANET.
- The mobile nodes themselves store and forward packets.
- This additional role of mobile node as routers leads to nodes incurring perennial routing-related workload and this consequently results in continual battery drainage.
- Energy spent can be substantially reduced by allowing the nodes to go into a sleep mode whenever possible.

## 4.5. Routing

- Packet routing is usually a much more complex task in adhoc network compared to that of an infrastructure-based network.
- The main complications arise on account of continual topology changes and limited battery power of the nodes.
- When the destination node is not in the transmission range of the source node, the route has to be formed with the help of the intervening nodes in the network.
- The purpose of routing is to find the best path between the source and destination for forwarding packets in any store and forward network.
- In traditional network, routing is a relatively easy task because the routes to nodes can be uniquely and efficiently identified based on the subnet structures encoded in IP.
- In a MANET, the nodes making up a route may themselves move or shutdown due to low battery energy.
- It is necessary to find a new route each time a node needs to transmit a message making routing an expensive and difficult task. Based on the above discussions,
    1. Traditional routing protocols would not be suitable in an ad-hoc network.
    2. Each node in an ad-hoc network needs to have routing capability and also needs to participate in routing to keep the network operational.

We can now state that MANET:

a) Forward the packet to the next node (hop).

b) While forwarding the packet, the sender needs to ensure that

i. The packets move towards its destination.

ii. The number of hops/path length is minimized.

iii. Delay is minimized.

iv. The packet loss is minimized.

v. The packet does not move around the network endlessly.

## 4.6. Essential of Traditional Routing Protocols

- It is necessary to have a clear understanding of the routing mechanisms deployed in a traditional network.

- Two important classes of routing protocols for traditional networks are the link state and distance vector.

- These two protocols are extremely popular in packet- switched networks.

- Both these protocols require a node to determine the next hop along the "shortest path" towards a given destination.

- The shortest path is computed according to some specific cost metric such as the number of hops in the route.

### 4.6.1. Link State Protocols (LSP)

- The term link state denotes the state of a connection of one router with one of its neighbours.

- A neighbour of a router is one in which it can be directly communicate without taking any help from the intervening routers.

- Each router determines its local connectivity information, and floods the network with this information with a link state advertisement.

- It stores this packet in a link state packet database (LSPDB). In addition to the routing table that each router maintains.

- Each router constructs the connectivity information for the entire network as a graph using Dijkstra's shortest path algorithm.

- Once a router constructs this graph, it computes the routing table from this and uses it in all its routing decision.

### *Characteristics of LSP*

Every router constructs a graph representing the connectivity between the various nodes in the network based on the information received from other routers.

- In a link state protocol, each router periodically determines the state of its links to its neighbours by exchanging hello packets with them across all its network interfaces.
- Based on the reply received from its neighbours, the router determines the state of the link in terms of the delay and other characteristics.
- The router forms a short message called the link state advertisement and sends it to its neighbours.
- A link state advertisement is also sent whenever a router experiences a connectivity change.

It contains:

- Identity of the router originating the messages.
- Identities of all its neighbours.
- The delay along various links to its neighbours.
- A unique sequence number.

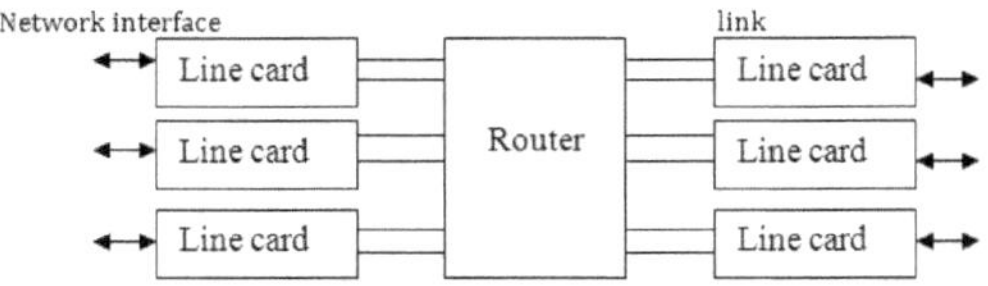


Fig. 4.2: Schematic Diagram of a Router

This link state advertisement is then flooded throughout the network as follows:

- A router sends a copy of a link state advertisement to all of its neighbours.
- A router receiving this message examines the sequence number of the last link state advertisement from the originating router by consulting its LSPDB.
- It replaces the last message with the currently received message in its LSPDB, and also forwards a copy of this link state advertisement to each of its neighbours.
- Dijkstra's iterative shortest path algorithm constructs the shortest path tree edge by edge, at each step adding one new edge corresponding to the construction of the shortest path to a router.
- A router maintains two data structures: a tree containing nodes which are node, and a list of candidates. This tree is essentially a shortest path first (SPF) tree. It first adds itself to the tree and thus is at the root.
- Once the network topology has been determined in the form of a shortest path tree, a router forms its routing table and uses it to find the best route to any destination.

- It can determine the optimal next hop for each destination in the network.
- Two widely used link state protocols in traditional networking are OSPF (Open Shortest Path First) and IS-IS (Intermediate System to Intermediate System).

### 4.6.2. *Distance Vector (DV) Protocols*

- Distance Vector Protocols get their name from the fact that they base their routing decisions on the distance to the destination in terms of the number of hops that a packet will have to traverse to reach its destination.
- The term vector means that routes are advertised as a vector (distance, direction) where distance is the number of hops between the two nodes and direction is defined as next hop router to which the packets need to be forwarded.
- The distance vector protocols are based on the well known Bellman – Ford Algorithm.
- The distance vector protocols share everything they know about the various routes in the network with their neighbours by broadcasting their entire route table.
- Each node advertises its entire routing table to its immediate neighbours only.
- A router transmits its routing table that has been formed from its own perspective.i.e represents the routes to various routers itself.
- For example, "router A is at a distance of five hops away, in the direction of the neighbour router X'.
- A number of techniques have been suggested to cope with instability and inaccurate routing information.
- The routers using the distance vector protocols do not have knowledge of the entire path that a packet would take to reach its destination. Instead ,they just know the following vectors:
  1. Direction in which a packet should be forwarded.
  2. Its own distance from the destination.
- The DV protocol is based on calculating the distance and the direction to any router in a network.
- They are two popular distance vector protocols are RIP (Routing Information Protocol) and IGRP (Interior Gateway Routing Protocol).
- RIP uses the hop count of the destination whereas IGRP takes into account the other information such as node delay and available bandwidth.
- RIP supports the cross-platform distance vector routing, whereas IGRP is a Cisco systems proprietary distance vector protocols.

- EIGRP is a distance vector protocols, it does not require transmitting updates periodically.
- Further updates are not broadcast and do not contain the full route table.

## 4.7. Popular Routing Protocols

We now discuss a few popular MANET routing protocols.

### 4.7.1. *Destination- Sequenced Distance Vector Routing Protocol*

- Destination- Sequenced Distance Vector Routing (DSDV) is an important MANET routing protocol.
- It is based on the table driven approach to packet routing.
- It extends the distance vector protocol of wired networks just as the traditional algorithm makes use of the classical Bellman-Ford routing algorithm.
- The avoidance of routing loops through the use of a number sequencing scheme.
- In DSDV, each node in a MANET maintains a routing table in which all of the possible destination and the number of hops to each destination are recorded.
- Hence, routing information is always readily available, regardless of whether the source node requires a specific route or not.
- Each node maintains information regarding routes to all the known destinations.
- The routing information is updated periodically.
- This can be considered a shortcoming of the protocol since it deprives a node from going into sleeping mode.
- Also, there is traffic overhead even if there is no change in network topology.
- Further, nodes maintain routes which they may never use.
- A sequence numbering system is used to allow mobile nodes to distinguish stale routes from new ones.

### *Important Steps in the Operation of DSDV*

- Each router in the network collects route information from all its neighbours.
- After gathering information, the node determines the shortest path to the destination based on the gathered information.
- Based on the gathered information, a new routing table is generated.
- The router broadcasts this table to its neighbours.
- This process continues till the routing information becomes stable.

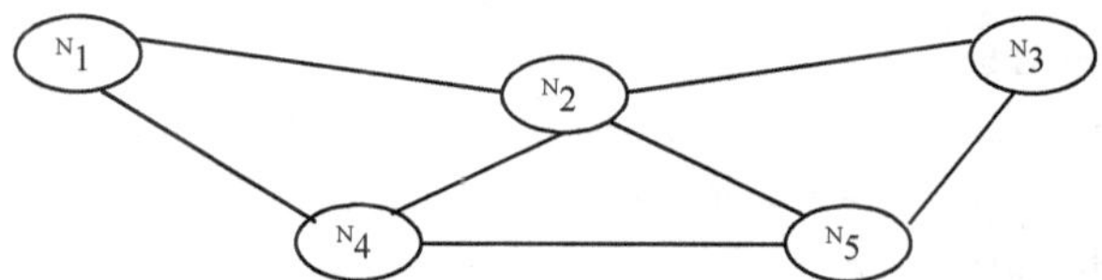

Fig. 4.3: Example of a MANET Topology at a Given Instant of Time

Table  DSDV Routing table for the MANET of fig.4.3

| Destination | Next hop | Metric | Sequence no | Install time |
|---|---|---|---|---|
| N1 | N1 | 1 | 321 | 001 |
| N2 | N2 | 1 | 218 | 001 |
| N3 | N2 | 2 | 043 | 002 |
| N5 | N5 | 1 | 163 | 002 |

## 4.7.2.  *Dynamic Source Routing (DSR) Protocol*

- It is a protocol was developed to be suitable for use in a MANET having a reasonably small diameter of about 5 to 10 hops and when the nodes do not move very fast.
- DSR is a source initiated on-demand routing protocol for ad-hoc networks.
- It uses source routing, a technique in which the sender of a packet determines the complete sequence of nodes through which a packet has to travel.
- The sender of the packet then explicitly records this list of all nodes in the packet's header.
- It is easy for each node in the path to identify the next node to which it should transmit the packet for routing the packet to its destination.
- In this protocol, the nodes do not need to exchange the routing table information periodically, which helps to reduce the bandwidth overhead associated with the protocol.
- Each mobile node participating in the protocol maintains a routing cache which contains the list of all routes that the node has learnt.
- Each mobile node also maintains a sequence counter called request id to uniquely identify the last request it had generated.
- DSR works in two phases are route discovery and route maintenance.

### Route Discovery

- It allows any host to dynamically discover the route to any destination in the ad-hoc network.
- When a node has a data packet to send, it first checks its own routing cache.
- If it finds a valid route in its own routing cache, it sends out the packet using this route.

- Otherwise, it initiates a route discovery process by broadcasting a route request packet to all its neighbours.

- The route request packet contains the source address, the request id and a route record in which the sequence of hops traversed by the request packet, before reaching the destination is recorded.

- A node forwards a route request message only if it has not yet seen it earlier, and if it is not the destination.

- The route request packet initiates a route reply upon reception either by the destination node.

- Upon arrival of the route request message at the destination, this information is piggybacked on to the route reply message that contains the path information and is sent to the source node.

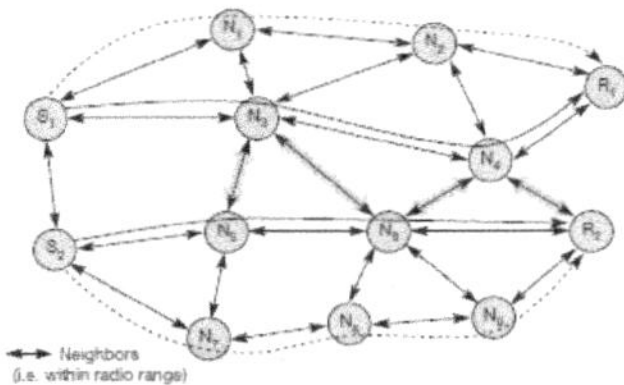


Fig. 4.4: Ad-hoc Network Topology

- Figure 4.4 shows an ad-hoc network topology. Sender S1 wants to send a packet to receiver R1, S2 to R2. Using the hop count as metric, S1 could choose three different paths with three hops, which is also the minimum. Possible paths are (S1, N3, N4, R1), (S1, N3, N2, R1), and (S1, N1, N2, R1). S2 would choose the only available path with only three hops (S2, N5, N6, R2). Taking interference into account, this picture changes. To calculate the possible interference of a path, each node calculates its possible interference (interference is defined here as the number of neighbors that can overhear a transmission).

- Every node only needs local information to compute its interference. In this example, the interference of node N3 is 6, that of node N4 is 5 etc. Calculating the costs of possible paths between S1 and R1 results in the following:

$$C1 = cost(S1, N3, N4, R1) = 16,$$
$$C2 = cost(S1, N3, N2, R1) = 15,$$
$$C3 = cost(S1, N1, N2, R1) = 12.$$

### Route Maintenance

- A known route can get broken either due to the movement of some nodes making up the route or battery of a node forming part of the route getting exhausted.
- Route maintenance is the process of monitoring the correct operation of a route in use and taking any corrective action when needed.
- When a host while using a route, finds that it is inoperative, it carries out route maintenance.
- Whenever a node wanting to send a message finds that the route is broken, it would help if it already knows of some alternatives routes.
- Since the nodes do not exchange any routing information in this protocol.
- If it has another route to the destination, it starts to retransmit the packet using the alternative route.
- Otherwise , it initiates the route discovery process again.

### 4.7.3.  Ad hoc On-demand Distance Vector (AODV)

- The route discovery and route maintenance activities in AODV are very similar to those for the DSR protocol.
- AODV does make use of hop-by-hop routing, sequence numbers and beacons.
- The node that needs a route to a specific destination generates a route request.
- The route request is forwarded by intermediate nodes which also learn a reverse route from the source to themselves.
- When the request reaches a node with route to destination, it generates a  route reply containing the number of hops required to reach the destination.
- All the nodes that participate in forwarding this reply to the source node create a forward route to destination.
- This route created from each node from source to destination is a hop-by-hop route.
- Recollect that DSR includes the complete route in packets headers.

### 4.7.4.  Zone Routing Protocol

- Zone Routing Protocol is a hybrid protocol.
- It incorporates the merits of both on-demand and proactive routing protocols.
- A routing zone is similar to a cluster.
- However, unlike clusters, zones can overlap.

- A routing zone comprises a few MANET nodes within a few hops from the central zone. Within a zone, a table –driven routing protocols is used.
- This implies that regular route updates take place only within a zone.
- Each node has a route to all other node within the zone.
- If a destination node happens to be outside the sources zone, ZRP employs an on-demand route discovery procedure which works as follows.
- When the destination node is reached in this process, a route reply is sent on the reverse path, back to the source.
- The source node uses the path saved in the route reply packet to send data packets to the destination.

### 4.7.5. *Multicast Routing Protocol for MANET*

- Multicast is the delivery of a message to a group of destination nodes in a single transmission as shown in figure.
- It is necessary to minimize the unnecessary packet transmissions as well as minimize the energy consumption.
- In order to achieve this, a multicast transmission should not be approximated by multiple unicast transmissions.

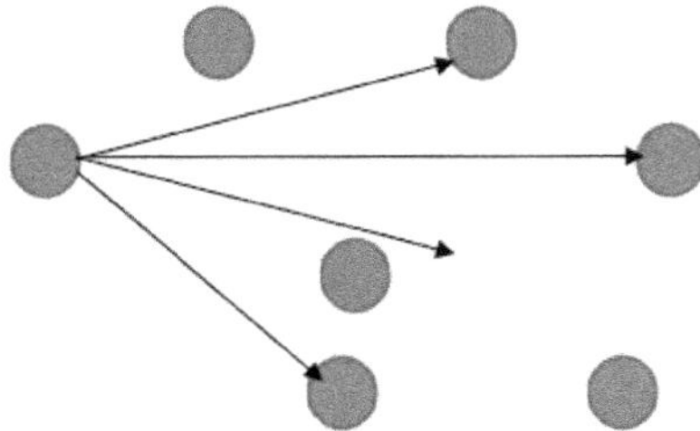

Fig. 4.5: Multicast Transmission

- Efficient multicast routing is much more difficult to achieve in a MANET compared to any other network.
- It is due to host mobility, broadcast nature of wireless environment and interferences from various noise sources.
- The proposed MANET multicast routing protocols either modify the conventional tree structure or deploy a different topology between group members.
- The popular MANET multicastings are either tree based or mesh based.

*Tree-based Protocol*

- Tree based schemes establish a single path between any two nodes in the multicast group.
- These schemes require minimum number of copies per packet to be sent along the branches of the tree.
- Hence, they are bandwidth efficient.
- However, as mobility increases, link failures trigger the reconfiguration of the entire tree.
- Examples: Multicast adhoc On-demand Distance Vector (MAODV).

*Mesh-based Protocol*

- Mesh based schemes establish a mesh of paths that connect the sources and destinations.
- They are more resilient to link failures as well as to mobility.
- The major disadvantage of this scheme is that multiple copies of the same packet are disseminated through the mesh, resulting in reduced packet Delivery and increased control overhead under highly mobile conditions.
- Examples:-On-demand Multicast Routing Protocol (ODMRP)

## 4.8.   Vehicular Ad Hoc Networks (VANET)

- It is a special type of MANET in which moving automobiles form the nodes of the networks.
- VANETs were initially introduced for vehicles of police, fire brigades and ambulances for safe travelling on road.
- In this network, a vehicle communicates with other vehicles that are within a range of about 100 to 300 meters.
- Multi-hop communication often results in rather large networks.
- In a city or a busy highway, the diameter of the network can be several tens of kilometres.
- Any vehicle that goes out of the signal range of all other vehicles in the network is excluded from the network.
- A vehicle that was outside the communication range of all other vehicles of a VANET can come in the range of a vehicle that is already in the network and as a result can join the network.

Few important uses of VANET are described below:

- A VANET can help drivers to get advance information and warnings from nearby environment via messages exchanges.
- A VANET can help disseminate geographical information to the driver as he continues to drive.
- Drivers may have the opportunity to engage in other leisurely tasks, such as VoIP with family, watch news highlights, and listen to series of media files known as podcasts.

## 4.9.    MANET Vs VANET

- A MANET is a collection of mobile nodes that communicate with each other over bandwidth constrained wireless links without any infrastructure support.
- VANET to be a special category of MANETs.
- The nodes are mobile in VANETs as well as in MANETs.
- However, the VANET nodes can communicate with certain roadside infrastructures or base stations.
- VANET is constrained to the road topologies; where as the movement of nodes in a MANET is more random in nature.
- MANET power is a major constraint but in VANET the battery power available in a vehicle is quite adequate.
- Relatively larger size of VANETs compared to MANETs.
- Relatively high speed with which vehicles move, need to be appropriately considered for the design of an effective VANET.

## 4.10.  Security

- MANETs are fundamentally different from both wired networks and infrastructure-based wireless networks.
- The problem of detecting and preventing anomalous behaviour.
- In a wired or wireless network, an intruder is outside the network and therefore could be controlled through a firewall and subjected to access control and authentication.
- In a MANET, an intruder is a part of the network and therefore much more difficult to detect and isolate.

A few important characteristics of adhoc networks that can be exploited to cause security vulnerabilities are the following:

## *Lack of Physical Boundary*

- Each mobile node functions as a router and forwards packets from other nodes.
- Network boundaries become blurred.
- The distinction between nodes that are internal and external to a network becomes meaningless, making it difficult to deploy firewalls or monitor the incoming traffic.

## *Low Power RF Transmissions*

- It is possible for a malicious node to continuously transmit and monopolise the medium and cause its neighbouring nodes to wait endlessly for transmitting their messages.
- Signal jamming can lead to a denial-of-service (DOS) attack.

## *Limited Computational Capabilities*

- Nodes in an adhoc networks usually have limited computational capabilities.
- It is difficult to deploy compute intensive security solutions such as setting up a public-key cryptosystem.
- Inability to encrypt messages invites a host of security attacks such as spoofing as well as several forms of routing attacks.

## *Limited Power Supply*

Since nodes normally rely on battery power, an attacker might attempt to exhaust batteries by causing unnecessary transmissions to take place or might cause excessive computations to be carried out by the nodes.

## *Characteristics of Secure Ad Hoc Networks*

Different types of attacks on the network attempt to breach one or more of these security features.

A secure ad hoc networks should have the following characteristics:

- **Availability:** It should be able to survive denial of service (DOS) attacks.
- **Confidentiality:** It should protect confidentiality of information by preventing its access by unauthorized users.
- **Integrity:** It should guarantee that no transferred message has been tampered with.
- **Authentication** : It should help a node to obtain guarantee about the true identity of a peer node.
- **Non- repudation**: It should ensure that a node having sent a message, cannot deny it.

# Review Questions

## *Part A*

1. Define Mobile ad-hoc networks?
2. What is hub, routers and base stations?
3. What is source and destination?
4. List out the characteristics of MANET?
5. List out the various application of MANETs?
6. List out the MANET design issues?
7. Define network topology?
8. Define Routing?
9. Define LSP?
10. Draw a schematic diagram of a router?
11. Define DV protocols?
12. What are the two popular distance vector protocol?
13. Define DSDV?
14. List out the important steps in the operation of DSDV?
15. Define Dynamic Source Routing Protocol?
16. What is Route discovery?
17. What is Route maintenance?
18. Define AODV?
19. Define ZRP?
20. What is multicast routing?
21. What is a tree-based protocol?
22. What is a mesh-based protocol?
23. Define VANET's?
24. List out the important uses of VANET?
25. Difference between MANET vs VANET?
26. What are the characteristics of ad-hoc networks?
27. What are the characteristics of secure ad-hoc networks?

## *Part B*

1. Explain the basic concepts of ad-hoc networks?
2. Explain the characteristics of Mobile ad-hoc networks (MANETs)?
3. Explain in detail about LSP?

4.   Explain in detail about DV protocols?

5.   Explain in detail about popular MANET routing protocols?

6.   Write a note on Vehicle ad-hoc networks (VANET's)?

7.   Explain in detail about security issues in MANET?

# Unit-5

## Mobile Platforms and Applications

### 5.1. Mobile Device Operating Systems

- Operating system is providing a set of services to the application programs.
- Operating system is usually structured into kernel layer and shell layer.
- The shell layer provides facilities for user interaction with the kernel.
- The kernel layer executes in the supervisor mode and can run privileged instructions that could not be run in the user mode.
- During booting, the kernel gets loaded first and continues to remain in the main memory of the device.
- The kernel is called the memory resident part of an operating system.
- The shell programs are usually not memory resident.
- The kernel of the operating system is responsible for interrupt servicing and management of processes, memory and files.
- The traditional operating systems such as Unix, and Windows are known to have a monolithic kernel design.
- The principle motivation behind this monolithic design was belief that in the supervisor mode, the OS services can run more securely and efficiently.
- Other hand, the main problems with the monolithic kernel design is that makes the kernel massive, non-modular, hard to tailor, maintain, extend, and configure.
- Considering the disadvantages of the monolithic kernel design, the microkernel design approach has been proposed.
- The microkernel design approach tries to minimize the size of the kernel code.
- The main advantage of this approach is that it becomes easier to port, extend, and maintain the OS code.
- The kernel code is very difficult to debug compared to application programs.
- The overall architecture difference between a monolithic kernel and microkernel architecture is schematically shown in figure 5.1.
- To restrict the size of the kernel of a mobile OS to the minimum, most mobile OS are to different extents, based on the microkernel design.

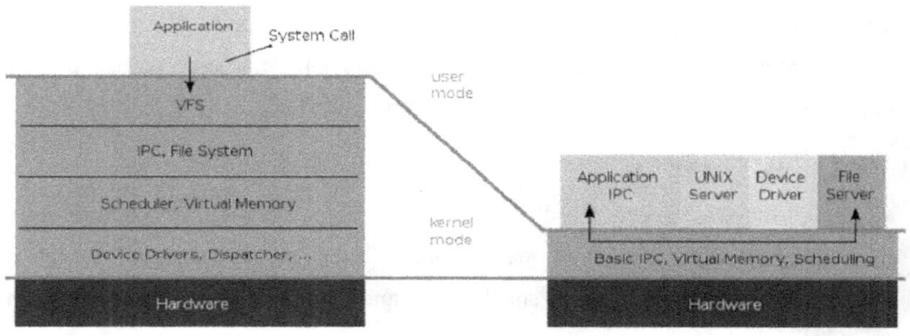


Fig. 5.1: Monolithic Kernel vs. Microkernel OS

## 5.2.    Special Constrains & Requirements

There are a few special constraints under which the operating system of a mobile device needs to operate.

### 5.2.1.  Special Constraints

The operating system for a mobile device needs to function in the presence of many types of constraints which are not present in a traditional computer.

***Limited Memory***

- A mobile device usually has much less permanent and volatile storage compared to that of a contemporary desktop or laptop.
- It provides a rich set of functionalities to meet user demands.

***Limited Screen Size***

- The size of a mobile handset needs to be small to make it portable.
- This limits the size of the display screen.
- Consequently, new innovative user interfaces need to be supported by the mobile OS to overcome this constraint and minimize user inconveniences.

***Miniature Keyboard***

- Mobile handsets either provided with a small keypad or the small-sized display screen is designed to be used as a keyboard in a touch screen mode using a stylus.

### Limited Processing Power

- A Vast majority mobile device incorporates ARM-based processors.
- These processors are certainly energy efficient, powerful, and cheaper compared to the desktop or laptop processors, yet these are significantly slower.
- Activities such as mobile application development that require use of memory-intensive utility programs, such as editors and compilers.

### Limited Battery Power

- Mobile devices need to be as lightweight as possible to increase their portability.
- Due to the severe restrictions that are placed on their size and weight.
- A mobile device usually has a small battery and often recharging cannot be done as and when required.
- The techniques used by an OS to reduce power consumption include putting the processor and display screen into sleep mode within a few seconds of inactivity and varying the intensity of transmitted antennae power as per requirement etc.,

### Limited and Fluctuating Bandwidth of the Wireless Medium

- The OS of a mobile handset needs to run complex protocols due to the inherent problems caused by mobility and the wireless medium.
- A wireless medium is directly susceptible to atmospheric noise, and thereby cause high bit error rates.
- Further, the bandwidth of a wireless channel may fluctuate randomly due to atmospheric noise, movement of some objects.
- Un-interrupted communication requires a special support for data caching, pre-fetching and integration.

### 5.2.2. Special Service Requirements

Several facilities and services that are normally not expected to be supported by a traditional OS are mandated to be supported by a mobile OS. We identify a few important ones in the following.

### Support for Specific Communication Protocols

- Mobile devices are often required to be connected to the base stations and various types of peripheral devices, computer and other mobile devices.
- This requires enhanced communication support.

- This type of communication protocols used for communication with the base station depend on the generation of the communication technology (1G,2G etc.,) in which the mobile device is deployed.

### Support for a Variety of Input Mechanisms

- A miniature keyboard forms the main user input mechanism for an inexpensive mobile devices.
- Sophisticated mobile devices ((smart phones) usually support the QUERY keyboard.
- Many recent mobile devices also support touch screen or even stylus based input mechanism along with the handwriting recognition capability.
- The different input mechanisms to be supported strongly influence the intended primary use of a device as well as specific customer segment for which it is positioned.

### Compliance with Open Standards

- Adhering to an open standard facilitates the development of innovative application by third-party developers.
- To facilitate the third party software development as well as to reduce the cost of development and time-to-market by the mobile handset manufactures, the OS should adhere to open standards.

### Extensive Library Support

- The cost effective development of third party applications requires extensive library support by the OS.
- It includes the availability of programmer callable primitives for email, SMS, MMS, Bluetooth, multimedia, user interface primitives and GSM/GPRS functionalities.

## 5.3.  Commercial Mobile Operating Systems

- It is a challenging task to design a mobile OS with a asset of core capabilities that are expected to be supported by mobile devices and with a consistent programming environment across all smart phones that install the OS.
- The mobile OS has to also facilitate third party development of application software and yet allow manufacturers of different brands of mobile devices to build their choice set of functionalities for the users.
- A few popular mobile OS are Windows Mobile, Palm OS, Symbian OS, Android etc.,

## 5.4. Software Development Kit

- The Android Software Development Kit (SDK) is a mobile application development framework using which developers can create applications for the android platform.

- SDK provides the tools and libraries necessary to develop applications that can run on android-based devices.

- An important advantage of android SDK is the low processor and RAM requirements.

- Android SDK can be installed on almost all common operating systems such as Windows, Mac OS, and Linux.

- The SDK comes with an Integrated Development Environment (IDE) and other tools which are required to develop applications.

- Android SDK converts Java byte code to Android Dalvik VM byte code.

- Eclipse can be used as the IDE which also automatically installs the android SDK as a Plug-in. After installing this plug-in, one can start the development of android applications.

### Features of SDK

It includes three main components:

- A client program which runs on the developers (called host) machine.
- A daemon program which runs as a background process on each emulator or device instance.
- A server program which runs as a background process on the host machine.

### Android Application Components

The following are the four components of an android application.

- Activity
- Each activity presents a GUI screen of an application.
- Content Providers
- It is used for reading and writing data that are either private to an application.
- Service
- It denotes a background task and not for interacting through a user interface.
- Broadcast receivers
- It responds to broadcast announcements by an application.

### *Advantages of Android*

- It is a open platform
- Android requires a low footprint of 250 KB.
- Modern design and is Easy to use
- Android supports robust

### 5.4.1.  Ios

- In jan 2007, Apple unveiled its sleek innovative mobile device.
- iPhone–causing a storm in the Smartphone marketplace.
- The iPhone was designed to replace Apple's highly successful ipod.
- Apple had developed iOS as iphone's Operating system was originally known as iPhone OS.
- iOS is a derivative of Mac OS.
- Mac OS was later extended for use in other apple devices such as iPod touch, iPad, and AppleTV.
- iOS is a closed and proprietary operating system fully owned  and controlled by Apple not designed to be used by various mobile phone vendors on their systems.
- Apple does not license iOS for installation on third-party hardware.
- For examples, user interactions with OS include gestures such as swipe, tap, pinch, and reverse pinch, all of which have specific definitions within the context of the iOS operating System.

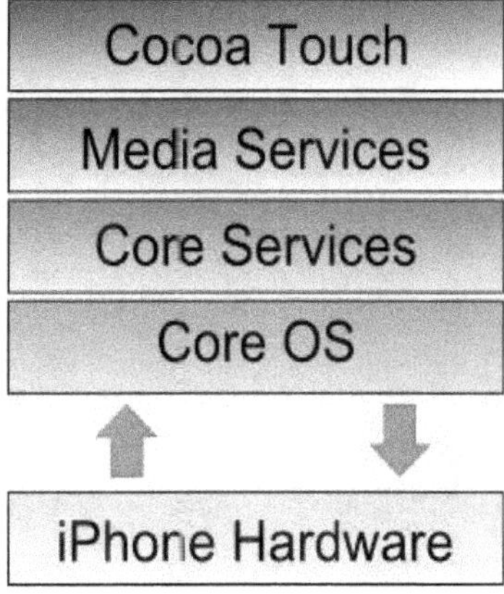


Fig. 5.2: iOS Architecture

### The Cocoa Touch Layer

- The Cocoa Touch layer sits at the top of the iOS stack and contains the frameworks that are most commonly used by iPhone application developers.

### Media Layer

- The role of the Media layer is to provide iOS with audio, video, animation and graphics capabilities. As with the other layers comprising the iOS stack, the Media layer comprises a number of frameworks which may be utilized when developing iPhone apps.

### Services Layer

- The iOS Core Services layer provides much of the foundation on which the previously referenced layers are built and consists of the following frameworks.

### OS Layer

- The Core OS Layer occupies the bottom position of the iOS stack and, as such, sits directly on top of the device hardware. The layer provides a variety of services including low level networking, access to external accessories and the usual fundamental operating system services such as memory management, file system handling and threads.

### 5.4.2. Android

- Android is an operating system based on the Linux kernel and designed primarily for touch screen mobile devices such as Smartphone's and tablet computers.

- The user interface of Android is based on direct manipulation, using touch inputs that loosely correspond to real-world actions, like swiping, tapping, pinching and reverse pinching to manipulate on-screen objects. Internal hardware. eg: accelerometers, gyroscopes and proximity sensors are used by some applications to respond to additional user actions.

- For example adjusting the screen from portrait to landscape depending on how the device is oriented.

- Android allows users to customize their home screens with shortcuts to applications and widgets, which allow users to display live content, such as emails and weather information, directly on the home screen.

- Applications can further send notifications to the user to inform them of relevant information, such as new emails and text messages.

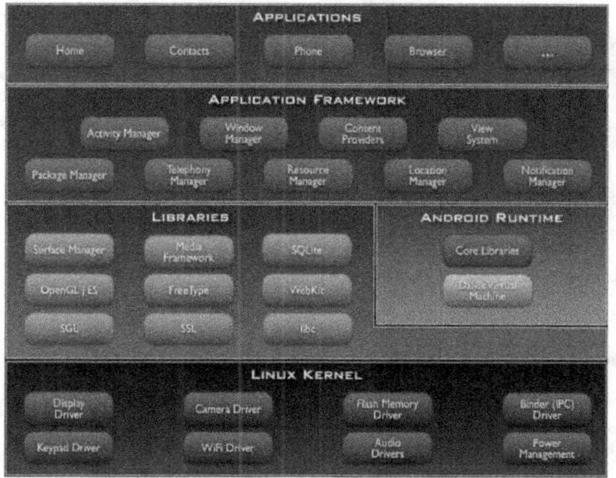


Fig. 5.3: Android Architecture

## *Application Layer*

- It is a set of basic application such as web browser, email client, SMS program, maps, calendar, and contacts repository management programs.

## *Application Framework*

- It provides a set of services that an application programmer can make use of it.
- Application Framework sits on top of native libraries, android runtime and Linux kernel.
- This framework come pre-installed with high-level building blocks that developers can use to program applications.

## *Libraries*

- The available libraries are written using multiple languages such as C and C++.
- These are called through a Java interface.

## *Runtime*

It consists of two components.

- A set of libraries provides most of the functionalities available in the core libraries of the java language.
- Other runtime is the Dalvik virtual machine.

### *Kernel*

- Android kernel has been developed based on a version of linux kernel.
- It does not support the full set of standard GNU libraries.
- This makes it difficult to reuse the existing Linux applications or Libraries on android.
- Android implements its own device drivers, memory management, process management and networking functionalities.
- Android is multitasking and allows applications to run concurrently.

### *5.4.3.  BlackBerry*

- Blackberry operating system is a proprietary operating system designed for Blackberry Smartphone's produced by Research in Motion Limited (RIM).
- Being a proprietary operating system, detail of its architecture has not been published.
- But, at the user level, the very good email system that it deploys is easily noticed.
- It supports instant mailing while maintaining a high level of security through on-device hardware-based message encryption.

### *5.4.4.  Windows Phone*

- The Important features of the mobile operating systems available from Microsoft.
- Microsoft Corporation developed an operating system in the year 1996 targeted specifically at these devices.
- This operating system has undergone several enhancements and modifications over successive generations.
- The main feature of windows CE operating System, which sets it apart from other traditional operating systems is the support that it provides for deterministic scheduling of time-constrained tasks.
- It was targeted for PDAs and not mobile phones.
- It was developed based on Pocket PC 2000 and was targeted specifically as an operating system for mobile phones which the different cell phone vendors can use in their cell phones.
- Consequently Windows mobile is now a family of three operating systems:
    - Windows Mobile Standard
    - Windows Mobile Professional
    - Windows Mobile Classic

- Windows Mobile standard and Windows mobile professional are targeted for use in smart phones. Windows Mobile Classic is not targeted for cell phones, but for PDAs.
- The evolution of Windows Mobile Operating System is schematically shown in fig 5.4

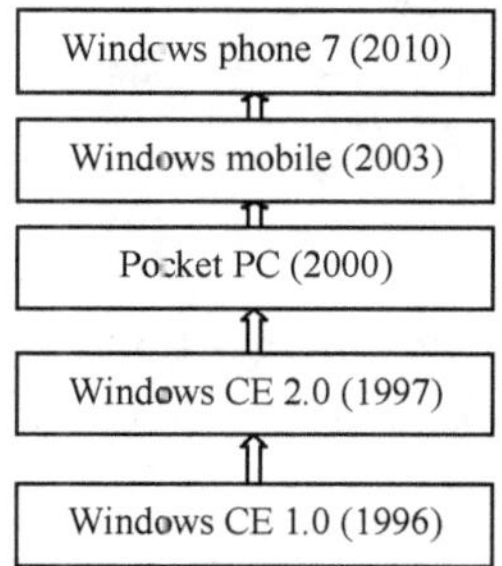


Fig. 5.4: Evolution of Windows Mobile Operating System

- They announced that windows phone 7 operating system would be used as the operating system for NOKIA Smartphone's.

A few important features of the windows mobile OS are the following:

- The Graphics/ window/Event manager (GWE) component handles input and output.
- It provides a virtual memory management.
- Supports security through the provision of a cryptography library.
- Application development is similar to that in the win32 environment.
- It does not provide true multitasking.

## 5.5.   M-Commerce

- Mobile commerce is an important application of mobile computing.
- Mobile commerce in simple words involves carrying out any activity related to buying and selling of commodities, services, or information using the mobile hand-held devices.
- M-commerce has over the last decade become extremely popular.
- The popularity of M-commerce can be traced to the convenience it offers both to the buyers and sellers.
- An important issue in M-commerce is how payments can be made securely and rapidly as soon as a buyer decides to make a purchase.
- Mobile payment is a natural evolution of E-payment schemes and has found an important place in M-commerce.

### Applications of M-Commerce

M-commerce application can be broadly categorized into either B2C or B2B.

### 5.5.1. Business-to-Consumer (B2C)

- Business-to-Consumer (B2C) is a form of commerce in which products or services are sold by a business firm to a consumer.

### Advertising

- Using the demographic information collected by the wireless service providers and based on the current location of a user, a good targeted advertising can be done.

### Comparison Shopping

- Consumers can use their mobile phones to get a comparative pricing analysis of a product at different stores and also the prices of the related products.

### Information about a Product

- Consumers can access additional information about products through their mobile phones.

### Mobile Ticketing

- Mobile phones can be used to purchase movie tickets called m-tickets using credit cards.

### Catalogue Shopping

- Mobile phones can be used to place orders for products listed in a catalogue.

### 5.5.2. Business-to-Business (B2B)

Business-to-Business (B2B) is a form of commerce in which products or services are sold from a company to its dealers.

### Ordering and Delivery Confirmation

- In this application, mobile phones can be used by dealers to order products.

### Stack Tracking and Control

- Mobile phones can be used to keep track of the stock in a distributed inventory system and send updates to a central database.

*Supply Chain Management(SCM)*

- Information about the supply chain processes can be made available via mobile devices.

*Mobile Inventory Management*

- An interesting new B2B application reported in envisages a "rolling inventory" consisting of multiple trucks carrying large amount of goods.

## 5.6.    Structure

- It providing a two set of programs: client side and server side.
- The client side programs run on the micro browsers installed on the users mobile devices.
- The server side programs performing database access and computations reside on the host computer (servers).
- The architecture of mobile commerce framework is shown in fig.5.5

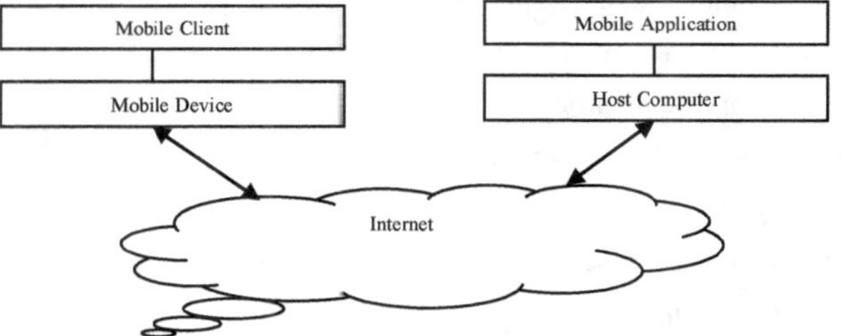


Fig. 5.5: Architecture of Mobile Commerce Framework

*Mobile Devices*

- Hand-held devices essentially present user interface to the mobile users.
- The users specify their request using the appropriate interface programs which are then transmitted to the mobile commerce application on the internet.
- The results are obtained from the mobile commerce application are displayed in suitable formats.

*Mobile Middleware*

- The main purpose of mobile middleware is to seamlessly and transparently map the internet content to mobile phones that may sport a wide variety of operating systems, markup languages, microbrowsers, and protocols.

- Most mobile middleware also handle encrypting and decrypting communication in order to provide secure transactions.

### Network

- Mobile commerce has become possible mainly because of the availability of wireless networks.
- User request are delivered either to the closest wireless access point or to a base station.
- Wired networks are optional for a mobile commerce system.
- However, host computers are generally connected to wired networks such as Internet.
- So user request are routed to these servers using transport and security mechanism provided by wired networks.

### Host Computers

- Host computers are essentially servers that process and store all the information needed for mobile commerce application.
- These applications usually consist of three major components: web servers, database servers, and application programs and support software.
- Web servers help interact with the mobile client.
- The database servers store data.
- The application program is the middleware that implements the business logic of the mobile commerce application.

## 5.7.   Pros & Cons

M-Commerce has its own advantages and disadvantages which are discussed below:

### Advantages

The following are the major advantages of M-commerce

- For the business organization, the benefits of using M-commerce include customer convenience, cost savings, and new business opportunities.
- From the customer perspective, M-commerce provides the flexibility of anytime, anywhere shopping using just a lightweight device.
- Mobile devices can be highly personalized, thereby providing an additional level of convenience to the customers.

*Disadvantages*

The following are the major Shortcomings of using M-commerce

- Mobile devices do not generally offer graphics or processing power of a PC.

- The small screens of mobile devices limit the complexity of applications.

- The underlying network imposes several types of restrictions.

## 5.8. Mobile Payment System

- Mobile payments are a natural evolution of E-payment schemes.

- A mobile payment may be defined as any payment instrument where a mobile device is used to initiate, authorize, and confirm an exchange of financial value in return for goods and services.

- Mobile devices include mobile phones, PDAs and any other device that connects to a mobile network for making payments.

- It is used for payment of bills with access to account-based payment instruments such as electronic funds transfer, Internet banking payments, direct debit and electronic bill presentment.

- An important issue which influences the establishment of the mobile payment procedure is the technical infrastructure needed on the customer side.

- A sophisticated technology may fail if the customer is not able to handle it with ease.

- On the other hand, simple procedures based on simple message exchange via short messaging services (SMS) may prove more successful.

- Some important problems dogging the M-payment schemes are security, privacy, and guarding against frauds.

### 5.8.1. Mobile Payment Schemes

Three popular types of M-payment schemes are currently being used:

- Bank account based

- Credit card based

- Micropayment

In each of these approaches, a third party service provider (bank, credit card Company, Telecom Company) makes a payment on the customer's behalf.

### *Bank Account Based*

- In this scheme, the bank account of the customer is linked to his mobile phone number.
- When the customer makes an M-payment transaction with a vendor or in a shopping complex, based on a Bluetooth or wireless LAN connectivity with the vendor, the bank account of the customer is debited and the values is credited to the vendor's account.

### *Credit Card Based*

- In the credit card based M-payment, the credit card number is linked to the mobile phone number of the customer.
- When the customer makes an M-payment transaction with a merchant, the credit card is charged and the value is credited to the merchants account.
- Currently, the penetration level of credit cards is rather low but is expected to grow substantially in the coming years.

### *Micropayment*

- Micropayment is intended for payment for small purchases such as from vending machines.
- The mobile device can communicate with the vending machine directly using a Bluetooth or wireless LAN connection to negotiate the payment and then the micropayment is carried out.
- Thus, the micropayment scheme is implemented through the cooperation of the mobile phone operator and a third party service provider.
- This approach has been used for vending from Coca-Cola machines.

## 5.9.   Security Issues

- M-commerce is anticipated to introduce new security and privacy risks beyond those currently found in E-commerce systems.
- Users of mobile devices can be difficult to trace because of roaming of the users.
- Also, mobile devices go on-line and off-line frequently.
- Thus attacks would be very difficult to trace.
- Another risk unique to the mobile devices is the risk of loss or theft.
- A mobile device that is stolen or has fallen into wrong hands can cause frauds that are difficult to track and prevent.
- A major problem in this regard is the lack of any satisfactory mechanism to authenticate a particular user.

## Review Questions

### *Part A*

1.  Define OS?

2.  Define mobile OS?

3.  What are shell layer and kernel layer?

4.  Difference between monolithic kernel and microkernel?

5.  List out the few special constraints and requirements in mobile OS?

6.  Define iOS?

7.  Define Android?

8.  What are the different layers in android?

9.  Define kernel?

10. Define blackberry OS?

11. What is windows phone?

12. List out the important features of wincows mobile OS?

13. Define SDK?

14. What are the features of SDK?

15. List out the four components of an android application?

16. List out advantages of Android?

17. What is M-commerce?

18. What are the applications of M-commerce?

19. Define B2C?

20. Define B2B?

21. Define client side and server side programs?

22. Draw an architecture of mobile commerce framework?

23. What is mobile middleware?

24. Define Host computers?

25. Difference between Pros and Cons of M-commerce?

26. What are mobile payment systems?

27. List out the three types of M-payment scheme?

28. What are the security issues in M-commerce?

## *Part B*

1.  Explain the basic concepts of mobile OS?
2.  Explain in detail about special constraints and requirements of mobile OS?
3.  Write a note on iOS?
4.  Explain in detail about android? With neat architecture diagrams
5.  Explain the SDK?
6.  What is M-commerce? List out the various types of application in M-commerce
7.  Explain the structure of mobile commerce?

9 789386 176752